Marketing Your Practice

*Creating Opportunities
for Success*

APA PRACTITIONER'S TOOLBOX SERIES

Marketing Your Practice

Creating Opportunities for Success

American Psychological Association Practice Directorate
with
Coopers & Lybrand, L.L.P.

AMERICAN PSYCHOLOGICAL ASSOCIATION
Washington, DC

A Cautionary Note:

This manual was written to serve both as a reference and as a tool to help providers practice more efficiently in a changing, demanding marketplace. The information contained herein is accurate and complete to the best of our knowledge. However, *Marketing Your Practice: Creating Opportunities for Success* should be read with the understanding that it is meant as a supplement, not a substitute, for sound legal, accounting, business, or other professional consulting services. When such services are required, the assistance of a competent professional should be sought.

First Printing, April 1996
Second Printing, September 1998

Published by
American Psychological Association
750 First Street, NE
Washington, DC 20002

Copies may be ordered from
APA Order Department
P.O. Box 2710
Hyattsville, MD 20784

Composition and Printing: National Academy Press, Washington, DC
Cover Designer: Leigh Coriale

Library of Congress Cataloging-in-Publication Data
Marketing your practice : creating opportunities for success / American Psychological
    Association Directorate with Coopers & Lybrand., L.L.P.
        p.   cm. — (APA practitioner's toolbox series)
    Includes bibliographical references.
    ISBN 1-55798-358-5 (alk. paper)
        1. Clinical psychology—Practice—United States.   2. Mental health services—
    United States—Marketing.   I. American Psychological Association.   Practice
    Directorate. II. Coopers & Lybrand.   III. Series
    RC467.95.M37   1996
    362.2'068'8—dc20   95-52584
                                                                                              CIP

British Library Cataloguing-In-Publication Data
A CIP record is available from the British Library

Printed in the United States of America

Contents

AMERICAN
PSYCHOLOGICAL
ASSOCIATION

Dear Colleague:

The American Psychological Association Practice Directorate is pleased to offer <u>Marketing Your Practice: Creating Opportunities for Success</u> as one component of the "APA Practitioner's Toolbox Series" written in conjunction with Coopers & Lybrand, L.L.P. This series of books is designed to help the practicing psychologist build a successful practice in an environment which requires attention to an increasingly complex approach to healthcare, while maintaining the quality of services for which psychology has become known. This specific book is intended to enable the practitioner to devise effective marketing strategies to increase competitiveness in the current healthcare climate.

Among the many changes which have occurred in healthcare is the increased reliance by both consumers and third-party payers on data and information to select services. Informed consumers expect to know enough about the services they seek to feel comfortable that help for their problems will be forthcoming. Third-party payers, whether employers, insurers, or the government, reasonably expect to know what services their beneficiaries will receive and the likelihood that treatment will be clinically effective and cost-effective. The success of a psychologist's practice will, in large part, be contingent upon the psychologist's ability to communicate this information to prospective purchasers. This communication is, generally speaking, the marketing of one's practice. Marketing is <u>not</u> synonymous with advertising, which may be but one small component of marketing.

On another level, marketing is part of the process of "growing" a practice. It involves determining the needs and goals of the practice, the needs of the consumer to be served and the objectives of the payer, and then designing a plan to successfully match those needs, goals, and objectives with the services to be provided. Marketing is not, of course, the panacea for solving all of a practice's problems in the currently complex healthcare environment. It is, however, a critical strategy for maximizing success, whether practicing in a solo or group practice and whether working within or apart from the third-party reimbursement system. Particularly within the third-party payment system, successful marketing will enhance practitioners' bargaining position in the healthcare market, and, in turn, increase their ability to exert influence over the way in which psychological services are provided.

Sincerely,

Russ Newman

Russ Newman, Ph.D., J.D.
Executive Director for Professional Practice

750 First Street, NE
Washington, DC 20002-4242
(202) 336-5913
(202) 336-5797 Fax
(202) 336-6123 TDD

Russ Newman, Ph.D., J.D.
Executive Director
Practice Directorate

Preface

Practitioners face new challenges resulting from the continually changing health care market reform initiatives that make it increasingly difficult to rely on the skills and strategies that served so well in the past. In addition to the American Psychological Association's continued advocacy against the threats of short-sighted efforts that sacrifice quality and outcomes for temporary cost savings, psychologists have an opportunity to develop and use the substantial bargaining power that can be achieved through collective creativity and energy.

This text is one in a series of publications dedicated to the concept that, by becoming better informed about the market changes occurring in health care today, practitioners can preserve quality of care and choose to participate in systems which recognize that the distinction between low cost and high value is the quality and outcome of care. Ultimately, systems that deny access to needed services in the name of cost control cannot succeed. Care may be postponed temporarily but only at an ever-increasing total cost that eventually must be paid.

Each of the topics included in this series was selected because of an increasing volume of requests received for information on the topic. Taken together, the series may assist practitioners in channeling energy into constructive strategies for achieving the goal of preserving quality in an evolving health care market. The complexities of today's behavioral health care environment necessitate an understanding of a topic of increasing importance in this competitive environment—marketing a practice.

MARKETING IN A CHANGING ENVIRONMENT

Some behavioral health care providers have a strong negative reaction to marketing. They may see marketing as a necessary (or unnecessary) evil that they are told they need to do in order to maintain a successful practice. The idea of marketing, however, should not conjure a vision of the "snake oil" salesman. Rather, marketing is simply communicating one's skills to potential clients and may be viewed as a process by which a behavioral health practice systematically determines the needs of its patients and potential patients and then develops a plan to meet those needs. The marketing process can be described in five steps:

1. Analyzing market opportunities
2. Selecting target markets
3. Developing marketing strategies
4. Developing a marketing plan
5. Implementing and controlling the marketing plan

Psychologists should market their practices to communicate to clients how they can service special behavioral health needs and to assist the practice itself in standing out from the competition. A well-planned and well-executed marketing strategy will increase the size of a practice, increase its financial stability, and help it meet its particular strategic goals. A marketing plan, like the entire marketing process, is not something a practice does once and forgets. It is an evolving process that results in periodic reviews and a revised marketing plan on no less than an annual basis.

The concepts presented in this text are equally applicable for the solo practitioner as for the group practice. Special emphasis should be paid to the sections that discuss a practice's "customers." Who are a practice's customers? Patients? Insurers? Managed care organizations? Government? Private-pay patients? Other practices? The answer may be one, some, or all of the above, depending on the nature of the practice, but, as a rule of thumb, anyone who either purchases or otherwise uses the services is a customer. The emphasis in this text is to explore new concepts in marketing a practice and to present strategies for applying them.

HOW TO USE THIS GUIDEBOOK

This guidebook is organized in a sequential manner. It leads the provider into developing a marketing plan with specific marketing strategies and tools. Before a practice can develop a marketing plan, however, it must go through other steps in the marketing planning process.

The first step in the process, analyzing market opportunities, is discussed in chapter 1. It shows a practice the importance of gathering information about its relative environment and outlines the components for analyzing a market: internal assessment, external assessment, consumer analysis, competitor analysis, and market research.

Chapter 2 discusses the second step in the marketing planning process—selecting target markets and market segmentation. This part of the marketing planning process involves forecasting the relative attractiveness of various markets. It also involves segmenting markets in a way that best suits a practice's needs.

After selecting and segmenting the market, the next step in the marketing process is developing a marketing strategy—the topic of chapter 3. Developing a marketing strategy involves determining a practice's long-range marketing objectives. It considers the life cycle of services as well as the position the practice wants to take with respect to other practices.

Developing the marketing mix is the focus of chapters 4 and 5. Chapter 4 begins with a discussion of the marketing mix elements of product, price, promotion, and place. Strategies and tools for product and pricing issues are discussed in chapter 4 and promotion issues in chapter 5.

Chapter 6 discusses the organization and implementation of a marketing plan. It provides a sample marketing plan and lists the steps necessary to implement and control the marketing process. Finally, it discusses a practice's ethical and social responsibilities in marketing, along with information on when and where a practice can find help in marketing.

Acknowledgments

This book was written by Tina E. Kind, MBA, of Coopers & Lybrand LLP. Ms. Kind is a consultant with Coopers & Lybrand's Health and Welfare Practice in Atlanta.

The following individuals from both the American Psychological Association and Coopers & Lybrand were instrumental in providing editorial assistance toward the successful completion of this work:

American Psychological Association
Russ Newman, PhD, JD
C. Henry Engleka
Chris Vein
Craig Olswang
Garth Huston

Coopers & Lybrand, LLP
Ronald A. Finch, EdD
Wanda Bishop
Alfred E. Schellhorn, MBA

1

Analyzing Market Opportunities

U NMET NEEDS *are everywhere. Stress, marital discord, and job insecurity, to mention only a few factors, result in increased need for psychological services. Traditional support mechanisms are diminished by the mobility and transitory nature of communities. Marketing is the psychologist's means of reaching out and communicating a willingness to help those in need. There are five steps to the marketing process: analyzing market opportunities, selecting target markets, developing marketing strategies, developing a marketing plan, and implementing and controlling the marketing plan. This chapter focuses on analyzing the market opportunities available to a psychology practice. It begins by looking inwardly at the practice to identify strengths. Next it discusses an external analysis, including evaluation of potential clients and the competition. Finally, there is a discussion of market research and its relevance to the marketing process.*

MARKETING IS A PROCESS

Put simply, a practice's goal in marketing is to improve patient access to professional care when a need arises. Plenty of need exists in the market that goes unmet for a variety of reasons. Societal constraints, for example, may restrict an individual's ability to obtain help when it is needed most. The objective of a marketing effort is to enable a person in need to find a practitioner efficiently. Marketing is the process for matching an individual in need with a practitioner.

Figure 1 illustrates the marketing process. The first step of the process is to analyze market opportunities. The objective is to gather information about individuals whose needs are currently going unmet. This process

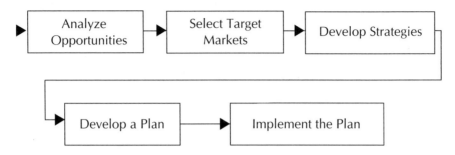

FIGURE 1   The marketing process.

may uncover information that leads a practice to target only some individuals and not others because of their specific needs (condition), ability to pay for services, or other factors.

Selecting the target market is the second step in the process. Once a practice has determined which individuals to target, a strategy needs to be developed to reach out to them in a manner consistent with professional ethics. This strategy is designed to be sensitive to individuals' needs, so that when an individual recognizes the need for services he/she can act on it appropriately. A plan is then developed that operationally divides the strategy into specific tasks that may be implemented. Finally, the marketing tasks are implemented.

GATHERING INFORMATION ABOUT THE RELATIVE MARKETING ENVIRONMENT

There are two major environments that affect providers' marketing plans: internal and external. Health care professionals must understand both in order to develop an effective marketing orientation and strategy. The internal environment deals with such issues as practice orientation and capabilities. A practice would not want to attract a clientele whose needs it cannot meet. The external environmental assessment develops an understanding of the local community and clientele. If the local neighborhood is largely composed of young families, an emphasis on learning disabilities is more likely to succeed than a geriatrics practice.

Components of market opportunity analysis are shown in Figure 2 and discussed in the following sections.

Internal Assessment	External Assessment	Consumer Analysis	Competitor Analysis	Market Research

FIGURE 2   Components of analyzing market opportunities.

INTERNAL ENVIRONMENT

An internal assessment begins with developing an understanding of the practice's services, how they are priced, how to promote them, and how to distribute them to customers (patients/clientele). Successful organizations are market driven; they identify what customers need and then design their services to meet those needs. Therefore, it is important to understand a practice's capabilities, strengths, and weaknesses in the marketplace. A successful marketing effort will increase practice activity in two ways. First, marketing activities demand time from practice members. Cultivating referral sources, developing plans, and writing marketing materials all require time and effort. Second, the practice may notice an increase in patient referrals. Increased intake volume will increase all aspects of the practice's business, including insurance filings and report writing. If the practice does not have the resources to serve additional clients, is marketing worthwhile?

It is important to understand that how a practice perceives itself may not be the same as how outsiders perceive it. A self-evaluation provides a realistic determination of the relative quality of the professional skills available within a practice. A sample professional skills assessment would ask the following questions:

- What services do we offer?
- Which services are particular strengths?
- Which services do we enjoy providing?
- What specialties do we have but do not emphasize?
- What additional services could we offer with more training, office support, or money?
- What special credentials or training do we have?
- What additional skills or credentials would improve our ability to serve potential patients?

Determining the mix of capabilities, skills, credentials, and training in a practice is a first step in assessing the internal environment. Second, the personal goals of the practitioners are important factors to consider. A sample personal assessment might ask:

- What do we want to do?
- What do we like about our practice?
- What do we not like about it?
- What would we change?
- What kind of patients do we prefer to treat?
- What types of treatment or methods do we prefer?
- When do we want to retire?

It may seem obvious that people should enjoy the work they do, but some people get so caught up in daily activities they forget to assess if they feel fulfilled. When members of a practice are assessing their personal goals, they need not limit the assessment to their clinical work. If members wish to spend a significant amount of time on community activities or with their families, that affects the assessment.

A practice may also conduct an assessment of the business skills available within the group. The business end of a behavioral health practice provides the support needed to deliver professional services. If members of a practice have business skills that are particular strengths, it is important to understand them and capitalize on them. Some sample questions a practice might ask about its business practices include:

- How efficiently and effectively is the practice managed?
- How much volume can it handle?
- Does it have excess or insufficient capacity?
- Is the practice barely paying the office rent?
- Is it able to float its reimbursement for several months or are prompt collections necessary to meet the next week's payroll?

Along with ensuring the survival of a practice, understanding its business and financial status is important from a marketing perspective in that different marketing activities require various amounts of time and money. For example, a press release announcing a new addition to a practice may only take a few minutes of time and no out-of-pocket money, but an advertisement in a local publication could be expensive. In addition, some practices may want to consider the opportunity cost of spending practitioner time on marketing activities instead of revenue-producing activities.

A practice's computer and information systems may assist in marketing (developing letters to past patients or referral sources). Practices may consider the following sample questions in performing an information systems assessment:

- Does the practice have computers?
- How comfortable is the staff with computers?
- Are the computers state-of-the-art?
- Are the names and addresses of referral sources recorded?
- Can letters be mail merged with the referral source list?
- If not, can address labels be produced?

If staff members are dissatisfied with the work environment, it may be difficult to attract and retain competent help, which in turn will detract from the success of the practice.

- Are records and accounts filed such that they can be retrieved quickly by anyone in the office?
- Is there an emphasis on confidentiality?
- Does the practice have many patient complaints?
- Is there a sense of camaraderie?
- Would the office stop functioning if one critical support staff member suddenly left?

EXTERNAL ENVIRONMENT

Over the past few years the health care market has experienced dramatic changes. In behavioral health the average length of a hospital stay has declined substantially, with not only an emphasis on outpatient care but also a reduced confidence in behavioral health counseling and providers because of the highly publicized acts of a few unethical individuals and organizations. The macroenvironment includes both opportunities and threats—uncontrollable forces faced by all practitioners. An external assessment may enhance a practice's understanding of how uncontrollable factors influence it.

Demographic Environment

Demographics include population size, population growth, age distribution, and ethnic mix. For example, a practice located near a retirement community may have no trouble attracting geriatric patients, while one near an elementary school may be more attractive to parents of children with attention deficit disorder. The following categories are particularly relevant to behavioral health practices:

- *Population age mix*—Because many mental health care providers segment their practices based on age, it is important to know if an individual segment is growing or declining in numbers. The age groups of teens, middle-aged adults, and older adults (over 65) are experiencing the most rapid growth in the United States, signaling a greater demand for services.
- *Ethnic markets*—While 80% of the U.S. population is white, the minority population percentage is increasing. The Hispanic population is estimated at 9% and is growing rapidly. The Asian population (currently about 3%) also is growing but is concentrated mainly in the far western United States. Each of these groups consists of unique subgroups that have specific needs, preferences, and purchasing habits.
- *Educational groups*—The U.S. population is somewhat polarized with respect to education. While 10 to 15% of the general population is considered functionally illiterate, the country also has one of the highest percentages of college-educated people (approximately 20%). Highly educated people have different demands and often prefer higher-quality services than their less educated counterparts.
- *Household patterns*—There seems to be no such thing as the average American household. Today's households include unmarried adults living together, singles living alone, single-parent families, childless married couples, and so-called empty nesters. No marketing approach can be expected to appeal to all groups.
- *Geographical population shifts*—As Americans migrate to the west and south, there has also been a move from urban areas to suburban areas. This shift affects practice location as well as influencing the distinct needs of urban versus suburban purchasers.

Practitioners can examine these forces in their local areas, as patterns and trends will vary considerably from area to area. To obtain such demographic information, a practice can check the following sources:

- Local office of planning and development
- Local office of building permits
- Other local and federal government offices
- Local board of education

- Local library
- On-line computer services

Economic Environment

Because operating a practice requires revenue, it is important to examine major economic trends, income distribution, savings, and debt. For example, if the nation or local area is experiencing an economic boom, there may be more opportunities for treating private-pay patients than when the economy is in a recession.

- *Economic trends*—There are numerous indicators of the general economic condition of the nation as well as one's local area. Among the major national indicators are the inflation rate, the rate of growth of the gross national product, interest rates, and changes in the stock and bond markets. Locally, the economy's health can be measured by the number of housing starts or the rate of loan/mortgage defaults.
- *Income distribution*—Real income per capita has not increased in the United States in the past 20 years, but there has been substantial growth in the number of two-income households. There is evidence that the rich are become richer, the middle class is shrinking, and the poor are becoming poorer. This effect is leading to a two-tiered market of affluent people who have little price sensitivity and working-class people who spend very carefully and purchase only necessary goods and services.
- *Savings and debt*—Consumer expenditures are also affected by the aggregate levels of consumer savings, debt, and credit availability. U.S. consumers save less (about 6%) than many other nations and have a high debt-to-income ratio. Providers must pay attention to any major changes in incomes, cost of living, interest rates, and savings patterns because such changes would also signal changes in the purchase of goods and services, particularly price-sensitive ones.

For information on the local economy, practitioners can check newspapers, the local chamber of commerce, the Better Business Bureau, local banks, and regional trade journals.

Technological Environment

One of the most dramatic forces shaping the world today is technology. The rate of technological change is accelerating. As personal computers, fax machines, and telecommunications evolve, more people will work at home and create more home-centered activity in general. This may have interesting social effects that would be of interest to behavioral health care providers. For example, there has been an increase in self-diagnosis as people gain ready access to laboratory technology (e.g., pregnancy test kits, cholesterol and blood sugar monitoring kits), as well as the Internet's references, databases, and forums. Psychological tests, often used by businesses as a screening device, are available on-line for those wishing rapid access to testing mechanisms.

Political Environment

There has been a substantial amount of regulation in the United States of businesses and business activities. Regulations serve several purposes: to protect companies from each other (laws to prevent unfair competition and predatory pricing), to protect consumers (truth in advertising laws, prevention of bait-and-switch pricing), and to protect the interest of society (charging businesses with the social costs created by their processes and products). Practitioners must be cognizant of the legal environment in order to operate in the most profitable and ethical manner. Confidentiality of records, mandates for reporting suspected abuse, and the threat of malpractice suits all affect practitioners.

Cultural Environment

The cultural environment may be important to some practices. Increased awareness of abusive relationships, for example, has encouraged more women to seek help in dealing with the aftermath of abuse.

Health Care Trends

The health care environment in the United States is constantly evolving. It is important to understand the relationships among providers, third-party payers, stakeholders, and the government. Knowing where they are coming from, what they think, and how they behave as a group, a practice can begin to learn how these trends impact it and how it can market itself to these payers.

- *Providers*—The various subsets of health care providers offer their own unique insights into the environment. Psychiatrists, counselors, and social workers in the mental health field all affect a psychologist's practice. There have been layoffs in the public sector that have pushed more mental health professionals into private practice. Providers not involved in managed care may see fewer patients as patients' choices are restricted by health maintenance organizations (HMOs) and other managed care organizations.

- *Third-party payers*—Third-party payers are entities that are not directly involved in either providing or receiving care but control payment for services. These groups generally include insurers, government, and employers.

  Insurance companies have had a major impact on health care delivery in the past, but there is much uncertainty about their ability to influence it in the future. In traditional fee-for-service medicine, the insurance company accepted the risk, determined the annual premiums it charged, and reimbursed providers as services were rendered. As health care costs spiraled out of control, there was great pressure on the insurers, among others, to control costs. The current trend is to shift the cost risk from insurers to providers, since providers ultimately make many of the spending decisions. There is also a trend among managed care organizations toward renting networks rather than building them.

  Insurers, however, began instigating the trend of managing health care costs with utilization review and case management programs. Today, some insurers see their role more as brokers than as risk-bearing entities.

  The federal and state governments, through Medicare and Medicaid, are another influential third-party payer. The federal government has been trying to stem the rise in Medicare costs for several years. The creation and proliferation of diagnostic related groups for acute hospitalization, resource-based relative value scales for physician services, and ambulatory patient groups for outpatient procedures have affected almost every aspect of health care delivery. These programs also influence the incentives for health care providers. Where the emphasis used to be on acute or invasive treatment, it is now on wellness and prevention.

Large self-insured employers continue to expect providers, particularly managed care organizations, to integrate the delivery of care into a seamless continuum of care. More progressive health care purchasers generally require networks of care that provide detailed credentialing of providers, simplified contracting, and seamless delivery. For patients this means a system of care in which they can be assured the same quality of care regardless of how they entered the system.

Additionally, patients continue to press the behavioral health care community to demonstrate and report efficiency and efficacy through periodic "report cards."

- *Stakeholders*—The changing face of health care has spawned a new generation of organizational entities that are one step removed from the health care triad of providers, patients, and insurers. Stakeholders can take many forms, as described in the APA Practitioner's Toolbox Series manual *Developing an Integrated Delivery System: Organizing a Seamless System of Care*. The most common are the HMO and the preferred provider organization (PPO).

The growth of HMO models (staff, group, foundation, independent practitioner association) has changed the entire practice and delivery of medicine. Reimbursement following renderence of services has been replaced by prepayment on a per-capita basis. As a holistic approach to preventing illness and controlling costs, HMOs have realized concepts and watched them proliferate throughout the health care system. HMOs have very high penetration in certain markets, such as California and Minneapolis, but are much less prevalent in other areas, such as the Southeast. They are on the leading edge of the managed care continuum and will probably continue to be the leader in innovative health care cost control and delivery approaches.

PPOs have been a bridge between traditional fee-for-service medicine ruled by the insurance companies and the full-blown managed care model of HMOs. As employers and the public pressure health care organizations to lower their costs, the approach that requires the least amount of change is the PPO. Although costs are controlled primarily through voluntary use of facilities that offer discounts, PPOs are a necessary link to more aggressive, and inevitable, forms of managed care.

CONSUMER ANALYSIS

In choosing a provider, the steps in a consumer's decision-making process include problem recognition, information search, and evaluation of alternatives preceding the purchase decision. As providers begin to market to patients, it may be helpful to understand the purchasing process (see Figure 3) as well as what stage a potential patient is in.

The purchasing process begins when a consumer recognizes a problem or unsatisfied need. He or she senses a difference between his or her actual state and the desired state that may have been triggered by an internal or external source. Often the first action taken by a consumer is an information search, which may be conducted on a passive level where the consumer simply pays more attention when the desired subject is brought up. The search can also be an active one in which the consumer seeks information from family, friends, or professionals such as a primary care physician or pastor. The amount and influence of the information depend on the service needed, the characteristics of the consumer, and the influence level of the informant.

Next, a consumer of behavioral health care services begins to evaluate alternatives; the consumer determines a preference among the various choices available. After a person has determined his or her preferences, he or she makes a decision to purchase a particular service. This text is designed to assist practitioners in developing strategies to effectively influence the consumer's final purchasing decision by positioning the practice in a favorable light early in the consumer's purchasing process.

COMPETITOR ANALYSIS

In addition to understanding the internal and external environments and customers' needs, a practitioner may also want to consider his or her

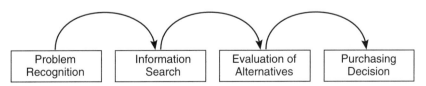

FIGURE 3   Consumer's buying decision process.

peers, colleagues, and competitors. In general, the marketing goal is not to win clients away from other professionals but to serve the needs of clients who are not currently receiving care. Therefore, a practice will want to determine what clients its peers already serve. Most successful practices design and implement a system for continuously gathering information about competitors through informal contacts, networking, and professional associations. Competitor analysis is not espionage. You simply want to develop a market strategy that reflects an awareness of other practitioners' specialties and clientele.

- Has the practice recently received a number of requests to transfer records to other local practitioners?
- Has the practice noticed announcements of new practices in the area?
- Have new members been added to the state's psychological association?
- Have existing psychologists broadened their scope to treat new patients?

A practice may believe it is easy to name its competitors, but each practice actually has a broad range of actual and potential competitors. There are four levels of competition:

- *Brand competition* is characterized by competitors who offer similar services to the same customers at similar prices. A practice that specializes in adult substance abuse might view itself as competing with other practices specializing in adult substance abuse but not as competing with practices that specialize in marriage and family counseling.
- *Industry competition* is characterized by viewing competitors in somewhat broader terms—all psychologists offering behavioral health services. A behavioral health practice, in this case, would view its competition as being all other psychology practices.
- *Form competition* is seen even more broadly as those organizations that offer behavioral health services. This would include psychiatrists and clinical social workers plus marriage and family counselors and community mental health centers.
- *Generic competition* is characterized by all organizations that compete for consumers' health care dollars. In this case, a psychology

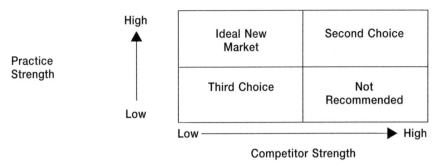

FIGURE 4   Competitor/Analysis.

practice may view its competition as being not just other behavioral health providers but also family physicians and self-help books.

If an internal assessment identifies a particular practice strength that consumers need and payers would cover, should the practice begin marketing the service? Obviously, the missing factor in the decision is whether competitors already offer the service. If strong competitors with sufficient capacity to meet clients' needs already exist in the market, the practice may not want to incur the costs of marketing that service. Figure 4 illustrates this analysis.

MARKET RESEARCH

Market research involves collecting information that is relevant to a specific challenge or opportunity facing a practice. Many firms, including those in the health care industry, undertake market research activities, and many of the techniques have become increasingly sophisticated and refined since they were first introduced. Market research consists of five major steps, as explained below.

Step 1: Define the Research Objectives

For market research the problem must not be defined either too narrowly or too broadly, for both will make the process more difficult and the results less useful. Not all research projects, however, can be made very specific. There are three types of research projects. The first is exploratory research, designed to gather preliminary data to suggest hypotheses for a problem or new ideas. The second type is descriptive research to determine magnitudes. For instance, how many people would pay for neuropsychological testing at various price points? The final type of research is causal, which tests a particular cause/effect relationship between variables. An example would be a survey to determine whether people might use a particular behavioral health practice if it offered evening hours.

Step 2: Develop the Research Plan

The second stage of market research involves developing a research plan, including decisions regarding data sources, research approaches, research instruments, sampling plan, and contact methods.

Data sources can be primary, secondary, or both. Primary sources are derived from direct research by the provider. Secondary sources consist of already published information. Because secondary sources are much less expensive to gather, people conducting research usually examine them first to determine if the problem can be answered at least partially from secondary sources.

Primary data can be collected through four means: observational research (observing relevant settings and persons), focus-group research (useful in conducting general exploratory research because it yields insights into perceptions, attitudes, and satisfaction), survey research (best suited for descriptive research), and experimental research (the most scientifically valid but can have a lengthy time frame).

Questionnaires are by far the most common instrument in collecting primary data for marketing. Telephoning subjects is good for gathering information quickly. The response rate is usually higher than that with mailed surveys, but the interviews must be short and not too personal, which could be a problem in conducting research about behavioral health practices. Finally, personal interviewing can be done. This is the most expensive method and requires more planning but is the most versatile and allows the interviewer to make additional observations regarding body language, dress, and so forth.

Step 3: Collect the Information

This stage of the market research process is usually the most expensive and subject to the most error. Numerous problems can arise. If surveys are used, some respondents will give dishonest or biased answers. Some interviewers may be dishonest. Researchers conducting experimental research must be careful not to influence the participants.

Step 4: Aggregate the Data and Analyze the Information

The next step in the market research process is to extract the relevant findings from the data. The researchers may apply decision models and statistical tools such as multiple regression, discriminate analysis, factor analysis, multidimensional scaling, or conjoint analysis. Optimization routines also can be performed, such as mathematical programming, statistical decision theory, game theory, or heuristics.

Step 5: Present the Findings

Whoever conducts the research should present the findings that are pertinent to decision making. Overwhelming decision makers with numbers will cause an entire marketing research effort to be wasted and will reduce the likelihood that management will conduct further market research in the future.

SUMMARY

There are five steps to the marketing management process: analyzing market opportunities, selecting target markets, developing marketing strategies, developing a marketing plan, and implementing the marketing plan. Analyzing market opportunities begins with gathering information about the internal and external marketing environments. A practice can assess its internal environment by examining its capabilities, strengths, weaknesses, financial status, and information systems in the context of personal and professional terms. A practice may assess the external environment, including demographics (population, age, ethnic mix); economics (inflation and interest rates, income distribution, savings, debt); and technological (computers, the Internet, home testing), political, and cultural trends. Behavioral health care providers should examine general health care trends as part of their external environment and to aid in planning.

One of the biggest marketing challenges is trying to understand consumers. A practice might examine how cultural, social, personal, and psychological factors affect consumer behavior. Consumers go through four steps in the decision-making process: problem recognition, information serarch, evaluation of alternatives, and purchasing decision.

CASE STUDY
Martin Clinic Analyzes Its Opportunities

The Martin Clinic is a small group practice composed of two full-time psychologists, one part-time psychiatric nurse, and a part-time clinical social worker. The office staff consists of one office manager/receptionist. Accounting, billing, and transcription services are handled by a management services organization affiliated with a local hospital. The practice has been stable for over 2 years but is now planning to add a third psychologist who does not have an established clientele. Therefore, a marketing plan is being developed for the practice. The first step, analysis of opportunities, has been completed by the practice administrator, Dr. Martin, with the following summary results:

Internal Assessment

The practice enjoys a strong reputation in the community for its work with adolescents with substance abuse problems. Although both psychologists speak frequently to community groups, the computer reports show that the social worker's contacts at the juvenile justice center and the high school are the primary referral sources for the practice. The office manager reports that adequate administrative support exists to handle increased volume; however, office space is a potential concern. The social worker voices resentment at being asked to share office space with the nurse.

External Assessment

Although the community continues to be affluent, the county commissioner has developed a plan to replace the current fee-for-service payment mechanism with a managed-care-type contract to provide support to the juvenile court. If implemented, this plan could potentially threaten practice referrals.

Consumer Analysis

When confronted with evidence of substance abuse by their children, parents reach a buying decision for behavioral health care services very quickly. The referral process depends on the ability to get a prompt appointment with a professional. Adding a provider will improve responsiveness to the perception of critical need.

Competitor Analysis

No other local practice specializes in adolescents with substance abuse problems. However, a general practice group has indicated an interest in the county contract.

Market Research

A survey of past patients indicates a high degree of satisfaction coupled with a strong preference for confidentiality, which serves to inhibit word-of-mouth and personal referrals. The survey also indicates that patients do not rely on the county's current payment system, instead preferring to use private insurance because of concerns that the county's records are not confidential.

Summary

The county's contracting initiative presents both an opportunity and a threat to the Martin Clinic. The market research may indicate that consumers would not accept a contracted therapist because of possible breach of confidentiality. Because of the pivotal role of its social worker, the clinic needs to resolve the office space issue immediately in a positive manner.

2

Selecting Target Markets and Market Segmentation

T HIS CHAPTER FOCUSES *on selecting and targeting appro-priate markets. A practice may know that it wants more pa-tients but may need to determine which ones or how to appeal to them. Using surveys might, for example, tell a practice that 50% of its current marriage and family counseling patients also want parenting work-shops. This part of the marketing process involves forecasting the rela-tive attractiveness of various markets. The second part of the chapter discusses market segmentation, or dividing the market into groups.*

The first question to be answered when targeting markets is the level of demand. Quantitative estimates are essential to analyzing market op-portunity, planning marketing programs, and controlling one's marketing effort.

MARKET DEMAND

Market demand can be divided into several different categories, in-cluding product levels and time ranges. Different product levels that would apply to a psychology practice include:

- service item, which is usually a specific procedure or service desig-nated by its current procedural terminology code;
- service form, which may be group therapy, individual counseling sessions, or testing services of the theoretical or conceptual basis of the practice;
- service line, such as substance abuse, adolescent services, or other specialization; and
- practice revenue, which is the summary or aggregate level.

Time levels include short range (less than 1 year), medium range (1 to 3 years), and long range (more than 3 years). Every demand estimate can be broken down into these levels, and each forecast has a different purpose. For example, if a practice wants to determine its office support staff requirements for the next month, it would want to estimate the short-term practice sales at the customer level. But if it were undergoing long-term strategic planning to determine whether it should recruit a new provider with expertise in a certain area, the practice may want to determine demand for a long-range service line.

The term *market potential* in this context refers to buyers who might exist for a particular service offering as defined by three characteristics: interest, capability, and access. Interest in a particular service is not sufficient to define a market. Potential consumers also must be able to afford the service. Capability is complicated by the fact that insurers and other third-party payers often pay part of patients' bills. In health care, consumer pay capability may be determined by whether an individual has health insurance coverage for mental health services and can afford the deductible and copayments. The final characteristic that defines market potential is access. If psychological services are not available in a certain area because there are no providers (e.g., remote rural areas), the market size is reduced.

Providers of psychological services have the choice of marketing services to the entire available market or concentrating on certain segments of it. A *target market* is a subset of the potential market that a practice elects to pursue. Total market demand is the total amount of services that *would* be bought by a defined customer group in a defined area. Practice demand is a group's share of the total market demand. In the case of psychological services, a practice's demand is the percentage of the overall amount of psychological services performed by that practice.

ESTIMATING DEMAND

Forecasting is the art of predicting what buyers are likely to do under certain conditions. It is usually very difficult to forecast demand for services, and the methods used range from crude and simplistic to highly sophisticated. Since psychological services are provided primarily by thousands of small practices, most practitioners have never estimated future demand or have done so only in a very crude way. Methods for estimating future demand are discussed below. Each method varies in its appropriateness with the purpose of the forecast, the availability of data, and the reliability of those data.

Survey of Buyers' Intentions

One effective means for determining future demand is to ask the consumers of behavioral health services. A phone survey can be administered to ask respondents about their intentions to use psychological services. Note that it may be difficult to administer a phone survey owing to the sensitive nature of mental health. Alternatively, physicians might be asked how likely they are to refer patients to psychologists in the near term compared to the recent past.

Expert Opinion

An easy way to forecast demand is to ask the experts. Experts may include consultants, trade associations, peers, and suppliers. Professional associations and journals often publish expert opinions regarding market demand.

Time-Series Analysis

This forecasting technique is based on an assumption that future activity is a function of past activity. This method involves dividing past patient revenues into various components: trends (basic developments in population and technology), cycles (periodic swings in activities), seasons (consistent movements up or down during certain times of the year), and erratic events (e.g., natural disaster, publicized suicide). An example follows.

> Past data show that the consumption of psychological services has been increasing at a rate of 5% annually. A practice's total number of sessions last year was 6,000. This year sessions should total 6,300, but the economy has taken a downturn and the numbers might be only 90% of what was expected (making the revised estimate 5,670). But demand for services increases around the holidays by 25%. Therefore, this quarter's estimates might be 1,771 (5,670/4 × 1.25).

MARKET SEGMENTATION

Market segmentation is the division of a market into distinct groups of buyers who act differently than other group of buyers but behave homogeneously within their segment. Different market segments may require different services or different marketing mixes. A practice's goal should be to identify ways of appropriately segmenting the market and then develop profiles of the resulting segments. Once that is accomplished, determining which markets segments are attractive to the practice is simplified with service positioning, which places services in a certain perceptual position in consumers' minds.

A segmentation strategy does not preclude a practice from offering certain services or accepting patients outside the marketing thrust. It simply means that a particular group of individuals is targeted for marketing.

Obviously, it would not be worthwhile to customize services to meet the needs of every consumer of psychological services. There are several common ways to accomplish segmentation:

- *Geographic segmentation*—The market is segmented according to where consumers live. If a high percentage of patients are in a few ZIP codes, this might serve as a useful segmentation variable, and marketing efforts could be directed at those who use a practice's services most. Advertisement dollars, for example, could be spent more effectively on an ad in a weekly community newspaper rather than the more expensive daily city paper.

- *Demographic segmentation*—The market is divided along personal characteristics such as age, sex, life stage, income, or occupation. These variables are easy to measure, and consumer wants, preferences, and usage rates are often highly associated with demographic variables. For example, a practice might want to target psychological testing of children or marriage counseling. With the demographic characteristics of market segments, marketing messages can address specific needs directly.

   Demographic variables are especially important for a psychological practice because patient services vary across those segments. Lower-income consumers may be less able to afford individual counseling unless they are insured or covered by Medicaid. Similarly, age is an important variable. Some psychologists limit their practices to children, for example. Practitioners can access children through a number of channels, such as schools, counselors, sports coaches, and family services. A less obvious variable is a disease or health-based one. Psychologists elect to segment the patient population based on the specific psychological services they consume, such as counseling for sexual abuse.

- *Behavioral segmentation*—The attitudes of patients toward psychological services are keyed on a number of behavioral variables, including user status (nonuser, exuser, first-time user, regular user), usage rate (light, medium, heavy), loyalty status (none, medium, strong, absolute), and benefits (quality, service, economy), to consider.

     Segmenting patients along the lines of benefits desired means dividing them into categories based on the benefits they seek from treatment. Marketing experts believe most health care consumers fall into four segments:
  1. *Quality*—patients who are unconcerned about costs and seek the best possible quality in the services provided.
  2. *Service*—patients who are not concerned about clinical quality as much as with being treated with respect and by someone with a caring, personalized attitude.
  3. *Value*—patients who look for a price/quality balance in deciding the value of a health care service.
  4. *Economy*—patients who are concerned only with the cost of services.
- *Segmenting referral sources*—Patients are divided according to their referral source. Some behavioral health care providers may want to concentrate on patients referred to them by the courts, school counselors, or physicians.
- *Multiple segments*—Patients are segmented according to more than one variable. In fact, there may be a strong correlation between some behavioral variables and demographic information, which may make it easier to target specific groups.

EVALUATING MARKET SEGMENTS

Once a practice has segmented the market, the next step is to evaluate the segments and determine which would be attractive to enter and target. Companies that manufacture consumer goods, for example, spend considerable time and effort collecting and analyzing data to best segment their market. For psychological practices, most of that effort is unrealistic, and the benefits received probably will not outweigh the costs. A more cost-effective approach would be to examine current patient records. What are the various ways they could be segmented? Keep the segments fairly broad, and concentrate on demographic, geographic, or behavioral attributes.

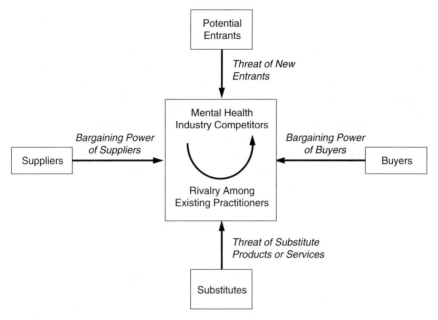

FIGURE 5   Factors determining attractiveness of market.

The first step in evaluating market segments is determine whether a segment has the right size and growth characteristics. Do not focus marketing efforts on a segment that is declining in size and historically unprofitable. Shown in Figure 5 are five forces that determine the long-term attractiveness of a market or market segment.

Industry Competitors or Segment Rivalry

A particular market segment may be undesirable if there are numerous, aggressive, or strong competitors. The scenario is worsened if the segment is stable or declining. Examples are eating disorders and geriatrics. If a practice is considering marketing a service but research on the external environment shows that several other practices offer the same undifferentiated service, the practice may want to reconsider.

New Entrants

A market segment may be less successful if it is likely to attract new competitors who attempt to gain market share. The likelihood of a new market entrant depends on the ease of entry, exit barriers, and likely retaliation. *Ease of entry* is a term that describes how quickly and cheaply a practice could enter a market. Variables that might affect ease of entry include capital requirements, economies of scales, and licensing requirements. Additionally, if integrated delivery systems dominate the market for behavioral health, a new small unaffiliated group may find that marketing a general practice is difficult. In the psychological services industry there is a medium ease of entry. Educational and licensing requirements are the strongest barrier to entry for psychologists and other behavioral health care providers. Beyond that a certain level of capital expenditures is required to set up a practice, but not nearly as much as in some other industries, such as manufacturing.

The term *exit barriers* refers to obstacles that impact an organization's ability to abandon a given market. Examples of exit barriers include legal, financial, or moral obligations to customers; government restrictions; lack of alternative opportunities; and low-asset salvage value. The psychological services industry has a low number of exit barriers. Providers, for the most part, can easily stop providing particular services.

The psychological services industry can be described as an attractive industry because there is a medium ease of entry and a low number of exit barriers. Specialties in the psychological services industry have a high ease of entry and a low number of exit barriers and therefore could be characterized by stable, low economic returns.

Threat of Substitutes

A market that has many potential substitutes is unattractive. The ability to substitute services limits the price that can be charged for those services. This issue, with respect to psychological services, depends on the individual service offering. A person may seek advice or counseling from sources other than psychologists, including clergy, friends, and untrained family members. Other segments, like testing, have a much lower threat of substitution.

Buyer Power

The higher the buyer power, the less attractive the segment is. Buyer strength can be influenced by a number of factors: buyer concentration and organization, a perception of overpricing, or undifferentiated services. Measures that buyers can take include trying to force prices down, demanding higher-quality services, and pitting competitors against each other. In segments involving psychological services the buyers' power is relatively low for services rendered to individual paying patients. On the other hand, if a significant portion of a practice consists of patients who are covered under contracts with one or two organizations, buyer power might be very high.

Supplier Power

The strength of the suppliers to a market segment may affect its attractiveness. With respect to psychological services, there is very little supplier power throughout the industry or in any segment because intellectual capital is the primary tool used for providing services. There is very little equipment other than office space needed for any service offering.

Examining the five forces that affect a segment's attractiveness is one more step in the market segmentation process. When a market segment appears to be attractive according to the five forces model, it should be considered in conjunction with the internal environment and strategic goals of the practice to confirm that the market aligns with the practice's overall objectives.

SELECTING MARKET SEGMENTS TO TARGET

After evaluating the various segments, which ones are targets? There are several patterns of selecting target markets, as discussed below.

Single-Segment Coverage

Several factors may cause a practice to focus on a single segment. A practice may *want* to focus on marriage and family counseling in an upper-middle-class suburb. It may be the service that is the most profitable, or no other competitors exist in the area, or marketing resources may be limited. Concentrated marketing can allow a practice to build knowledge of a particular segment, learn more about unmet needs, and build a reputation in that area. The risks for concentrating on a single segment are higher, however, because the segment could suddenly be reduced or eliminated or a new competitor may enter the segment.

Multisegment Coverage

In this case a practice selects a number of different segments to target, but there is little synergy between the segments, and each is attractive independently of the others. This strategy has an advantage over the single-segment strategy in that the practice diversifies its risk. If one targeted segment becomes undesirable, the organization may still remain profitable by targeting the other segments.

Product Specialization

This strategy involves the organization obtaining specialized training and certification to permit concentration on providing a certain product or service to various segments. A psychological services example is testing. In this case the practitioners would offer testing services to a number of different groups. The advantage of this strategy is that the practice builds a reputation and expertise in a certain product area. The disadvantage is the downside risk that would occur if the service was superseded, became outmoded, or lost its benefit coverage.

Market Specialization

Here, the organization serves all the needs for a particular customer group. A psychological services example would be an adolescent specialist. The psychologist would target all needs only for adolescents. This strategy's advantage is that a practice gains a strong reputation for serving a customer group that is often easily identifiable, but the disadvantage is that of being susceptible to changes such as a decline in segment size (the number of adolescents), regulations, or insurer budget cuts in health plan coverage.

Full-Market Coverage

This strategy involves attempting to serve all customer groups with all products or services in a given market. A large integrated delivery system, for example, might undertake this strategy successfully, but most practices are not big enough to adopt this strategy.

One way to devise a segmentation strategy is to develop a matrix of services, as shown in Figure 6. Note on the matrix the services offered by competitors and substitutes. Then mark the current position of the practice. Unmarked cells are potential segments. It is easier to target adjacent

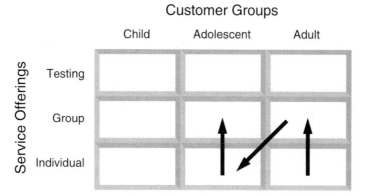

FIGURE 6   Segment entrance strategy.

cells rather than jump from one corner of the matrix to another. In other words, a practice that has specialized in testing children is more likely to be successful at expanding into other services for children or testing for other age groups than it would be at changing both the age group and services simultaneously.

SUMMARY

Selecting target markets, the second step in market planning, involves forecasting the attractiveness of various markets and dividing them into segments to make the marketing effort most effective. A practice can estimate demand by using a variety of methods to determine which market segment might be the most attractive to enter. The most popular method is by consumer survey, but expert opinions and time-series forecasts also may be used. A practice evaluates market segments to determine which would be best to target. One evaluation tool is to examine the five forces that determine the long-term attractiveness of a market: industry competitors, threat of new entrants, threat of substitutes, buyer power, and supplier power. There are several patterns that practices can use to select target markets: single segment (e.g., marriage/family counseling), multisegment (marriage/family counseling and individual counseling), product specialization (testing), market specialization (adolescents), and full market coverage (all people and services).

CASE STUDY
Martin Clinic Selects a Target Market

Having performed an analysis of opportunities, Martin Clinic proceeds with the next step in the marketing process—selecting its target market—with the following results:

Demand Forecast
Based on the number of qualified referrals the social worker could have made to the practice if more capacity existed, sufficient demand currently exists to support the addition of 2.3 psychologists to the practice. Discounting this number to reflect the percentage of referrals who do not make contact with the practice adjusts the demand to 1.8 additional professionals.

Market Segmentation
Outcome data developed by the clinic indicate more positive results with clients who are younger at the time of intake. Client surveys indicate a strong preference for the highly confidential, caring atmosphere of the Martin Clinic, located on a side street in a private freestanding office building. Approximately 85% of the clientele have health insurance coverage for behavioral health services. Of those, half are insured through one of the four insurers with which Martin Clinic has a PPO agreement.

Target Market
Martin Clinic decides to target those potential clients who are insured by one of the PPO groups it is affiliated with. It decides not to pursue the county's business because of the potential for a negative reaction from the existing client base, which values the confidentiality of a private practice and is willing to forgo county assistance.

3

Developing a Marketing Strategy

T HIS CHAPTER FOCUSES *on developing a marketing strat-*
egy based on evaluations of the internal and external environ-
ments. A marketing strategy requires an understanding of a practice's
strengths, weaknesses, threats, and opportunities. It allows the practice
to focus its marketing efforts in concert with its overall goals. This chap-
ter discusses methods of differentiation for a practice as well as strategies
that a practice can use for the various life cycle stages of a service. Fi-
nally, strategies are examined that practices can use depending on their
role in the marketplace: market leader, market challenger, market fol-
lower, or niche player.

The third step in the marketing process—developing a marketing
strategy—occurs after market opportunities, target markets, and market
segments have been examined. The options for differentiating services
are explored in order to identify those that will help the practice develop
and sustain a competitive advantage in the marketplace.

METHODS OF COMPETITIVE DIFFERENTIATION

Differentiation is the act of designing a set of meaningful differences
to distinguish a practice from its competitors. Although some consumers
may see psychological services as a commodity with no differences among
providers, there can actually be substantial differences in outcome, theoretical approach, and cost. Patients have different needs and require different services.

The primary means of differentiating a practice in a market is through service that exceeds customer expectations. Although provider expertise and competence are two important aspects that may differentiate a psychological practice from its peers, many patients are unable to distinguish the technical competence of providers and must base their opinions on other measures they can more readily identify. These factors include:

- *Credibility*—The provider is perceived to be trustworthy. One can be credible without being competent.
- *Attitude*—Staff members are respectful, considerate, and courteous. Patients are treated as though they are important to the practice.
- *Reliability*—Services provided to patients are consistent, accurate, and timely. Appointments are kept in a timely manner.
- *Responsiveness*—Any problems, concerns, or questions patients have are handled promptly and efficiently.
- *Communication*—The staff try to understand patients' needs and communicate clearly with them using appropriate terminology.
- *Confidentiality*—Patients are confident that information is protected from unauthorized use.
- *Image*—Even when two practices offer identical services, patients may perceive different images. An image can take years to evolve, and one advertisement or logo change will not change a practice's image overnight.

DEVELOPING A POSITIONING STRATEGY

Positioning is the act of designing a practice's service offerings and image so that a distinct and valuable impression is made in patients' minds. Developing a positioning strategy includes three steps:

1. identifing any services, personnel, and image differences between the practice and its competitors;
2. deciding which differences are most important to patients; and
3. effectively communicating to the target market the differences and advantages of the practice. (Communication strategies are discussed in Chapters 4 and 5.)

An important positioning strategy is to promote a consistent message. For example, a practice negotiating with a large employer to provide an employee assistance program may find that its cost efficiency message is enhanced by describing its evening hours in terms of absenteeism rather than convenience. Even a practice's location and decor can support or undermine the positioning strategy of the practice.

LIFE CYCLE

An important aspect of developing a marketing strategy involves consideration of the "life cycle" of a potential product or service. Many services have a life cycle that requires different marketing strategies over time. Sometimes, the underlying psychological condition continues to exist, but the treatment goes through a life cycle (see Figure 7). The events that precipitate the change from one stage to another might be evolving technology (such as new clinical procedures) or a change in public perception. Several decades ago few providers treated eating disorders. Today, there is a much higher awareness level, and the demand for those services has leveled off. By understanding where disorders and services are in their life cycle, a practice can plan and develop strategies more effectively.

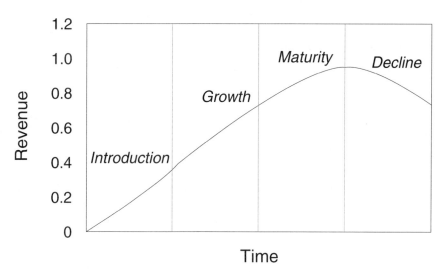

FIGURE 7   Life cycle stages. Adapted from *Marketing Management* (6th ed.; p. 349) by P. Kotler, 1988, Englewood Cliffs, NJ: Prentice-Hall. Copyright 1988 by Prentice-Hall. Adapted by permission.

Many psychologists will never have an opportunity to launch a new service, but some may. Examples include a practice that enters a joint venture with a local home health agency to expand into the geriatric home-bound market for behavioral health services, the psychologist who contracts with a charity organization to test disruptive children for disabling conditions, and the therapist who expands his or her experience in testifying in child custody cases into a consulting practice that provides the family court with an unbiased opinion.

STRATEGIES FOR THE LIFE CYCLE STAGES

The *introduction* stage begins when a new service is launched, which takes time. Marketing costs at this time are usually high and patient visits low. Psychologists who are on the leading edge of developing new therapies or in other ways providing services in their introductory phase may be inclined to accept some financial risk. The service may prove to be clinically successful, but it may not be accepted by referral sources, payers, or patients.

There are several marketing strategies for promoting services in their introductory phase, including the following:

- *Rapid penetration* involves promoting a service heavily and charging a low price. This strategy allows a practice to gain market share when patients are largely unaware of the service.
- *Slow penetration* involves providing a new service at a low price with little promotion. This strategy makes sense when a practice believes there are many potential patients, patients are sensitive about price, and there is potential competition among providers.

The *growth* stage is marked by a rapid increase in revenues. More patients begin purchasing the service. More providers begin offering it. There may be new features, expansion, or changes to the service offering. It is not uncommon for demand to exceed supply. Prices for the service remain level or decline slightly as demand increases. A practice's promotional activities may stay the same or increase slightly, and there is new competition and a continual effort to educate the market. Generally, the providers who benefit most during a service's growth stage are the ones who introduced it to an area. Practices that acquire new providers or ignore other services to concentrate on this one service may experience problems once the demand for that particular service levels off.

There are several strategies for providing a service in its growth stage.

In this stage a practice should try to strengthen its competitive position by using some of the following techniques:

- Improve the service based on initial patient feedback.
- Add additional services that complement the practice's primary services.
- Introduce the service to new market segments.
- Lower the price to attract more price-sensitive patients.

Maturity is the stage in which the demand for a service slows and the service enters a stage of steady demand. Eventually, a peak is reached and patient demand may begin to fall. Remember, the time frame for each service and each life cycle stage is different. Products or services that are fads can race through the entire life cycle in less than a year. Other products and services spend decades in the maturity stage. During the maturity stage, a practice cannot grow as a result of increasing demand; it must grow by increasing market share relative to the competition.

There are numerous strategies for services in the maturity stage:

- Expand the number of patients consuming services by promoting to potential patients, entering new market segments, and converting the competition's patients.
- Modify the service by improving the quality or improving features.
- Modify the marketing mix by changing the product, price, promotion, and distribution characteristics.

The *decline* stage is characterized by reduced numbers of patients and sessions and declining revenue. Reasons for decline include technological changes, changes in patient acceptance, changes in patient preference, or increased competition. However, as revenues begin to decline, some practices may withdraw from offering the service entirely. The remaining providers may reduce the market segments they target and their prices.

Depending on competitive strengths and the service's attractiveness, a practice can undertake the following strategies in the declining stage of the life cycle:

- Identify a weak service by analyzing volume, profit, and cost data.
- Increase promotion as competitors drop the service.
- Drop the service to focus on other, more profitable ventures.

STRATEGIES FOR MARKET LEADERS, CHALLENGERS, FOLLOWERS, AND NICHE PLAYERS

Classifying a practice according to the role it plays in its particular market can help form appropriate marketing strategies. Practices can be classified four ways, each with different goals and appropriate strategies.

The *market leader* is the practice with the largest market share in the relevant market. It usually leads other practices in introducing new services and strongly promotes its activities. The market leader may not be revered or respected, but it is at least acknowledged as an orientation point. While being the dominant practice has obvious advantages, the market leader must exert effort to remain in a dominant position. Other practices constantly challenge the dominant one, and without continuous effort, it can easily lose market share. It might spend too much and hurt profits, spend too little and be overtaken, or appear outdated compared to newer companies.

For a dominant practice to remain number one, it has several strategic options:

- *Expand the total market demand*—When a total market expands, the dominant practice in the market is usually the one that benefits most. The market leader should seek new users, new uses, and more usage.
- *Defend market share*—The market leader must continually defend its market share from competitors. Sometimes competitors will band together against the leader. The best response from the leader is continuous innovation.
- *Expand market share*—Another way to improve profitability is for the market leader to increase its market share. Market research has shown that market share can be a key variable in profitability.

The *market challenger* is a practice that is second, third, or lower in market share. It can adopt one of two major strategies: vie to become the dominant leader through an aggressive bid for market share (making it a market challenger) or be content in maintaining its current position (making it a market follower). A practice that is attempting to become the dominant one must define its strategic objective (usually to gain market share). It can do that in one of three ways: challenge the market leader, challenge practices its own size that are weak or underfinanced, or challenge smaller practices that are weak or underfinanced.

A *market follower* is a practice that is not the dominant one and is not trying to become it. Following can be a very profitable position to take. The strategy of product or service imitation rather than innovation makes sense for many organizations with limited resources to devote to research and development. If two practices both try to dominate a market, the battle for market share may result in one being driven out of business or both having reduced profits.

There are three basic strategies for a market follower. The first is to mimic the leader's services, distribution, and promotion. The second is to imitate the leader by copying some aspects while maintaining a small level of differentiation. Third, a follower can act as an adapter by offering its services to different markets to avoid direct competition with the dominant practice.

Rather than being a follower in a large market, a practice can be a leader in a smaller market, otherwise known as a *niche* player. In this case, a practice specializes in market segments of little interest to the dominant practices. Even organizations with low total market share can be highly profitable by using a niche strategy. An example might be a psychology practice that focuses on the Medicaid population.

SUMMARY

A marketing strategy requires determination of long-range objectives to allow a practice to focus its efforts. Differentiation is designing a practice's service offerings to create a distinct impression in the consumer's mind. It involves identifying the differences between a practice and its peers, deciding which of those differences are most important to patients, and communicating those differences. Some services go through a life cycle that requires different marketing strategies at different stages. Four distinct roles exist for a practice: market leader, market challenger, market follower, and niche player.

CASE STUDY
Martin Clinic Defines Its Strategy

Martin Clinic's partners met in closed session to define a marketing strategy in response to the report outlining the opportunities and target market. Dr. Martin presided over the meeting and reviewed the results of the prior sessions. The following describes key conclusions from the meeting:

- Martin Clinic is differentiated from its peers by several factors, including:
  - *Competence*—The clinic specializes in the treatment of adolescent substance abusers.
  - *Confidentiality*—All records are maintained privately with no potential for public access as may occur under a government contract.
- The service offering continues in a growth cycle with increased reports of teenage drug and alcohol use.
- Martin Clinic serves a niche market since it dominates this service line without direct competition but does not attempt to provide service outside this specialty.

4

The Marketing Mix, Service, and Pricing Strategies

MARKETING IS THE PROCESS *of identifying the needs of consumers and offering services in a form, at a place, and at a price they desire. It also includes making consumers aware of services and showcasing their value. This chapter delineates the difference between marketing and advertising, terms sometimes erroneously used interchangeably. It discusses the elements of the marketing mix and gives a detailed discussion of service and pricing strategies.*

Advertising is one small part of a marketing effort. Advertising is nonpersonal communication through various media (e.g., Yellow Pages), usually paid for by the identified sponsors. Marketing, an overall strategic effort, affects a practice's characteristics, offerings, and quality of services by responding to consumer needs and desires. Regardless of a practitioner's clinical ability, demeanor, and skill, patients will not use the services if they are not aware of them, the services are not offered at convenient or acceptable times, the services are not offered at a suitable or convenient location, or the services are not perceived to be fairly priced and affordable. To meet these conditions a practice must devise a marketing strategy and develop a marketing plan to meet its objectives.

THE MARKETING MIX

In developing a marketing strategy, it is important to understand basic marketing nomenclature. Marketing professionals often refer to the "four Ps" when discussing the types of decisions to be made in a marketing effort. The marketing mix is the specific combination of these four items developed to meet a practice's marketing objectives:

- Product/service
- Pricing
- Promotion
- Place (distribution)

Product/Service

Product decisions concern the specific services a practice offers. To make these decisions, an understanding of the current environment and the business must be developed. Specifically, the following questions must be answered:

- Who are the patients?
- Which patients are wanted?
- What services will attract those patients?

The services offered include several items. Obviously, the clinical offerings are the most critical component. Some less obvious aspects, however, also affect the service offerings. The physical attributes of the practice—the external appearance of the building, the reception area decor, and the condition of any public areas—all contribute to perceptions about the office. In addition, the appearance and demeanor of the psychologists and support staff are part of the product mix. For example, confidentiality may be a concern to patients if a sign-in log or facsimile machine is visible in the reception area. Strategies for the product element are discussed in detail later in this chapter.

Pricing

Pricing decisions concern the cost of services. This part of the marketing mix can be more difficult for psychology practices because of the addition of third-party payers into the pricing arrangement. Pricing decisions are based on a number of factors. One important consideration of the pricing decision is the effect of insurance reimbursement. Accepting only private-pay patients may be a practice's decision. Depending on the focus of the practice, pricing decisions made in conjunction with managed care organizations (HMOs, PPOs) can have a significant impact on a practice's ability to attract and retain patients.

In financial terms, services should be priced in a way that will maximize profits. If services are priced too high, the large revenue per patient will be offset by low volume. Conversely, if prices are too low, there will be ample volume, but overall revenue will not be as high.

Another perspective upon which to base pricing decisions is market share. Numerous studies have shown a strong correlation between market share and overall profit. Pricing services at the market level eliminates price as a differentiating factor, and other aspects of the practice will be evaluated by consumers. Competing for patients shifts to criteria such as quality of service and convenience of location. Being the high-priced provider in a market is the final pricing option. This strategy may be optimal if services are in high demand and patients are willing to pay a premium for them. Although in other industries consumers usually perceive higher-priced goods and services as being of superior quality, this perception may not be applicable to health care.

Promotion

Promotion is the art of communicating a service to potential and actual customers. There are four major tools used to communicate a service offering. Advertising is a paid form of nonpersonal communication by an identified sponsor. Promotion is a short-term incentive to encourage the purchase of a product or service. Public relations is designed to improve, establish, or protect a company's image. Finally, personal contact is an oral presentation to prospective purchasers. (Chapter 5 provides a detailed discussion of promotion strategy.)

Place

Where and when to offer services involves choosing a location and office hours that support strategic goals. For example, a practice might market services to affluent, self-paying patients in an area convenient to them. For low-income patients, proximity to public transportation may be critical. Satellite, storefront, and shopping center locations are options. In addition, staggered or extended office hours appeal to working patients. Other aspects to consider are adequate, convenient parking and easy access for handicapped people.

SERVICE STRATEGIES

Psychology practices provide services rather than tangible goods. There are several unique characteristics that affect the marketing efforts of a service organization.

Intangibility

Unlike products that can be seen, tasted, smelled, heard, or felt before purchase, services are intangible. A patient undergoing individual therapy cannot predict the outcome of the service received. To reduce their uncertainty, patients will look for evidence of the quality of the service and draw conclusions from the location, people, environment, communication, and price they see.

When marketing a psychological practice, the task is to include as much palpable and material evidence of the service offerings as possible. The physical setting will help convey information.

Inseparability

Unlike tangible goods that are produced at one point and consumed at another, services are usually produced and consumed at the same time. In the case of a psychology practice, the psychologist (producer) and patient (consumer) are present at the same time. The provider-patient interaction is a special feature of marketing a service because both the provider and the patient affect the outcome.

Variability

Providing psychological services is highly variable, depending on who, when, and where they are provided. Every psychologist has different skill levels and competencies. Even the same individual will provide varied services depending on the time of day, mental energy, and mood.

Perishability

There is no inventory for services. Providers sometimes bill their patients directly for missed appointments because of the associated opportunity cost. The value of the service exists only at the point of the patient's appointment. This is not a problem when demand for services is steady because services can be staffed in advance. It becomes more difficult when demand fluctuates. There are several strategies a practice can use to produce a better match between supply and demand. The reservation/appointment scheduling system can be used. Of course, emergencies occur that change the best-laid plans, but strict control over the process will eliminate many problems and unhappy patients. Peak-time efficiency routines can be developed. Support staff might perform only essential tasks during peak patient periods. Slower times can be used to catch up on noncritical activities.

Marketing Strategies for Service Organizations

Service organizations have traditionally used marketing less than manufacturing firms have. Small service businesses may have no formal management or marketing activities. Professional organizations once considered it unethical to market their services. Most psychology practices employ less than 10 providers and, until 1978, it was unethical, if not illegal, to market health care services. Although a portion of the psychology profession still believes marketing is inappropriate, marketing activities are becoming widely accepted as an educational and communications approach to reaching out to clients in need.

The marketing approach for service organizations is more difficult to manage than that for a product because of intangibility, inseparability, variability, and perishability, as described above. Some marketing experts contend that marketing a service requires not only external marketing but also internal and interactive marketing. External marketing is the normal marketing activity a practice undertakes—determining the marketing mix of product, price, promotion, and place. Interactive marketing is the employees' skill in serving their customers. Patients judge the quality of the service provided not only by its technical quality but also by its functional quality.

Determinants of Service Quality

Several factors that consumers use to determine service quality are listed below. A patient survey can greatly help a practice determine its patients' perceptions of the quality of services provided. In order of importance, the five determinants of service quality are:

1. *Reliability*—the ability to perform services dependably and accurately.
    - Are the services necessary and appropriate?
    - Is the provider reasonably accessible?
2. *Responsiveness*—the provider's willingness to provide prompt service.
    - Are appointments made within a reasonable time?
    - Are complaints resolved quickly?
3. *Assurance*—the knowledge and courtesy of employees and their ability to convey trust and confidence.
    - Is the response rate to surveys high?
    - Is the word-of-mouth referral rate high?
    - Do people communicate complaints anonymously?
4. Empathy—the provision of caring and individualized attention.
    - Does the staff appear concerned about the patients?
    - Are questions answered respectfully?
    - Are unexpected waits explained to patients?
5. *Tangibles*—the appearance of the physical facilities, personnel, and communication materials.
    - What does the office look like?
    - Are professional licenses and degrees displayed?

Common Practices of Well-Managed Service Companies

Practices that have a true service commitment and customer focus can easily differentiate themselves among their peers. Listed below are common practices among well-managed service companies:

1. *Strategic concept*—a clear sense of the customers and consistently meeting their needs.
    - Does the practice solicit patient feedback and input?
2. *History of management commitment to quality*—focus on service performance as well as profits and income.
    - Do complaints and suggestions result in tangible changes?
3. *Setting high standards*—challenging benchmarks and striving to meet them.
    - Does the practice set performance benchmarks for service or outcomes?
    - What are the procedures for responding to patient complaints?
4. *Systems for monitoring service performance*—audit service perfor-

mance through customer surveys, suggestion forms, and service-audit teams.

- Are referral sources surveyed for feedback?

5. *Procedures for satisfying customer complaints*—quick and generous response to complaining customers.
   - What are the procedures for responding to patient complaints?
6. *Satisfying staff as well as customers*—good staff relations reflect positively on customer relations.
   - Are staff concerns given attention and merit?

Gaps Between Perceptions and Expectations

Psychologists and patients have varying expectations for services. Perceptions can vary as well. If perceptions meet or exceed expectations, the result is a satisfied patient and provider. If perceptions fall below expectations, a practice must identify where the gap took place in order to correct it. Patient surveys and other market research can help a practice identify gaps.

Strategies for Improving Patient Satisfaction

Satisfied patients are helpful to a practice in two ways. They continue to use the practice, and they give free word-of-mouth advertisement for the practice, which often results in increased referrals. There are numerous strategies for improving patient satisfaction. A practice can adopt the ones that best match its time, available funds, comfort level, and appropriateness to the services being provided.

- Call patients, especially those with significant problems, one or two days after a visit, to see how they are doing.
- Call patients or providers (when authorized to do so) if they have been referred elsewhere to check on their status.
- Create a practice patient panel—patients who meet with the practice semiannually or quarterly to give feedback and suggestions.

Strategies for Informing Patients About the Practice

Patients may become anxious at the thought of going to a psychologist. They may have no way of deciding if behavioral health services are needed, whether they are priced correctly, or whether receiving services will help them. Informing patients about the practice may ease their fears.

- Develop a brochure that explains the practice, its services, and financial policies. (This is discussed in detail in Chapter 5.)
- Mail copies of the brochure to current patients and new patients before their first scheduled appointment.
- Warmly welcome new patients.
- During the patient's first visit, discuss the provider's view of behavioral health care as well as the patient's view.
- Give a new patient time during the initial appointment to ask questions about the practice and its providers.
- As long as appropriate, ensure that a patient understands what services are being provided, what the intended outcome is, how the conclusion was arrived, and how follow-up care will be delivered.
- Ensure that everyone in the practice has good listening skills.
- Ask the patient if he or she has any questions.

Pricing Strategies

Price, the second element of the marketing mix, has its own unique characteristics. Price is the only element of the marketing mix that affects revenue; the other elements produce costs.

Patients interpret price changes differently. A price cut may be interpreted as a sign that the practice is in financial trouble or that the quality of services has been reduced. Some patients interpret price increases as evidence of a more desirable service, that the service represents an unusually good value, or that the practice is trying to take advantage of its clients.

A practice considering a price increase must also consider its peers' reactions. They are most likely to react to price changes when the number of practices offering the same service is small, the service is homogeneous, and the consumers are highly informed. In the example of behavioral health services, an oversupply of providers in the area and the competitive relationship among them will influence consumer reaction.

SUMMARY

A practice's marketing strategy is determined by its strategic goals, while its marketing mix consists of the four Ps: product/service, pricing, promotion, and place (distribution). There are several unique issues associated with marketing behavioral health services: intangibility, inseparability, variability, and perishability. One way for a practice to differentiate itself is to deliver services that are of higher quality in terms of reliability, responsiveness, assurance, empathy, and tangibles.

CASE STUDY
Martin Clinic Sets Its Marketing Mix

During its strategy and planning meeting (described in Chapter 3), the Martin Clinic also confirmed its marketing mix:

- *Product/service*. Martin Clinic will provide treatment for substance abuse by adolescents, with priority on meeting the needs of potential patients insured by one of the PPOs that the clinic has contracted to serve.
- *Pricing*. Martin Clinic shall abide by the terms of its contracts. For noncontract clientele, a fee schedule will be maintained that is 20% higher than the highest PPO allowance. The clinic will continue to participate in Medicare and Medicaid as a public service.
- *Promotion*. The clinic will work through its PPOs to promote its services.
- *Place*. The clinic will modify the interior space of its offices to provide privacy to *all* professionals and their clientele.
- No changes in service or outcome measurement processes are to be adopted.

5

Promotion

FOLLOWING ON *the product and pricing aspects of the mar-keting mix's four Ps is the element of promotion. Promotion is the tool that practices use to communicate their service offerings. There are a number of promotional tools that fall into the major categories of advertising, promotion, public relations, personal contact, and direct marketing. This chapter describes the various promotional tools and strategies to help a practice determine its best promotion mix.*

Since marketing is communication, it is important to understand how communication works. Senders of communications must know what audiences they want to reach and what responses they want to achieve. Senders must transmit their messages through efficient media that reach their target audiences. They must also develop feedback channels so they can know receivers' responses to their messages.

STEPS IN DEVELOPING EFFECTIVE COMMUNICATIONS

There are six major steps in developing effective communications:

1. Identifying the target audience.
2. Determining the communications objectives.
3. Designing the message.
4. Selecting the communications channels.
5. Establishing a promotion budget.
6. Determining the promotion mix.

Identifying the Target Audience

The target audience may be potential patients, current patients, decision makers, or referral sources. The audience can number from one person to small groups to large groups (like at a seminar) or the general public. The target audience is a critical influence in decisions to be made regarding the message, how it is communicated, when it is communicated, and where it is communicated. The right message communicated to the wrong audience can show poor results.

One major part of analyzing an audience is to assess its current image of the practice, its products, and its competitors. Image is the set of beliefs, ideas, and impressions that a person has of a practice or service. One step to gauging a target audience's knowledge of a practice is to use a familiarity scale. People are asked to respond to five categories of familiarity: never heard of, only heard of, know slightly, know a fair amount, or know very well. If most people respond to the first two choices, the practice's first challenge is to build awareness of its services.

Suppose a practice wants to create an image that is different from its current image. It must decide what image gaps it has and which ones it wants to close. Does the practice want to portray the quality of its care, cost effectiveness, facilities, or friendliness? Next, it must ask itself how changing one particular aspect would favorably affect its overall image. What communication strategy would close the gap? What would the cost be? How long would it take?

Changing a practice's image is a long process. An image can persist long after a practice has changed for the better or the worse. Image persistence is explained by the fact that once people have a certain image, their future perceptions are consistent with that image. It takes highly contrasting information to raise doubt and cast a new image in people's minds.

Determining the Communications Objectives

After its target audience is identified, a practice needs to determine its communications objectives. The practice might be seeking to plant an idea in the patient's mind, change the patient's attitude, or get the patient to act. There are six buyer awareness states that patients go through in the decision-making process:

1. *Awareness*—The task is to create awareness of a practice's services or simple name recognition. This can be accomplished by repeating the name of the practice or the services it offers.
2. *Knowledge*—The task is to make people who are aware of a practice more knowledgeable about the services it offers.
3. *Liking*—If people are aware and knowledgeable about a practice

and its services, the next task is to develop favorable feelings about the practice.

4. *Preference*—Because people may like a practice's services does not mean that they prefer them. The next task is to encourage a preference among people for a practice's particular services.

5. *Conviction*—Preference for a service is followed by developing conviction. The objective here is not only to ensure a preference for your practice but also conviction (movement) toward purchasing or selecting its services.

6. *Purchase*—Consumers may have a preference for a practice's services and may even have some conviction about the purchase, but circumstances may cause a delay in the purchasing decision. Ultimately, a practice wants consumers to develop the conviction and actions necessary to make a purchase.

Designing the Message

After determining the desired audience response, the next step is to develop an effective message. The message should gain and hold the target audience's attention, arouse desire, and elicit action. The message content should denote some kind of benefit motivation, identification, or reason why the audience should consider or investigate the practice. The message may contain rational appeals to the customer's self-interest, an emotional appeal, or a moral appeal to the customer's sense of right and wrong.

Selecting the Communications Channels

There are two major types of communications channels: personal and nonpersonal. A personal communications channel involves two or more persons communicating directly with each other through face-to-face interaction, by person to audience, or through the mail. The major advantage of personal communication is that the presentation is individualized and feedback can be considered.

Personal channels can be divided further as shown in Table 1. Contacting buyers directly at a seminar on stress reduction is an example of personal contact. Speaking to a family practice group on recognizing potential abuse is an example of promotion. Speaking to a cancer support group is an example of public relations.

TABLE 1   Communication Channels

Personal Communication			Nonpersonal
Promotion Tools	Public Relations	Personal Contact	Advertising Tools
Letters to referral channels	Speeches	Educational presentations	Newspaper ads
Health fairs	Seminars		Brochures
Trade shows	Charitable donations		Educational booklets
Exhibits	Sponsorships, publications		Leaflets
Demonstrations	Health and wellness events		Directories
	Lobbying		Symbols
	Articles in company magazines		Logos

Word-of-mouth referral is especially important to health care providers. There are numerous occasions when people ask others for recommendations. If they have confidence in the person giving the recommendation, they normally act on it. Service providers have a strong interest in building referral channels. Psychologists get referrals and recommendations from physicians, clergy, school counselors, and social workers. The challenge for providers is to locate several referral sources that produce high yield and take action to cultivate their support. Developing a relationship with referral sources is an important priority for behavioral health providers.

Nonpersonal communication channels carry messages without personal interaction. They include media, "atmospheres," and events. Print media consist of newspapers, magazines, and direct mail; broadcast media are radio and television; and display media include billboards, signs, and posters. "Atmospheres" are packaged environments that create or reinforce customer tendency to purchase a given service. Office decor is an example of this form of nonpersonal communication. Events are occurrences that communicate a particular message.

Personal communication is usually more effective than mass communication. Mass communication affects personal attitudes and behaviors through a two-step process of flowing ideas to the decision makers in market segments and then from the decision makers to others.

Establishing a Promotion Budget

Promotion budgets vary considerably among industries, ranging from virtually zero up to 50% of revenues for certain types of companies (e.g., cosmetics). There are four major methods to determining a promotion budget:

1. *Affordable method*—This method consists of answering the question, "How much can I afford?" It ignores the role of promotions as an investment in the long-term success of an organization and the short-term impact on volume.

2. *Percentage of revenue method*—This method consists of setting promotional expenditures as a specified percentage of total practice revenues. The advantage of using this method is that it encourages management to think about the relationship between promotion cost, price, and profit; it also encourages competitive stability. The disadvantages, however, outweigh the advantages. The method uses circular logic by viewing revenue as a cause for promotion rather than promotion as a cause for revenue. Second, it discourages innovative promotion programs. Finally, it does not encourage planning the marketing mix relationships. Therefore, it is not normally a recommended method.

3. *Competitive parity method*—This method consists of spending the same amount on promotion as one's competitors do. While some people claim this helps prevent promotion wars, this is not the optimal method, and there is no evidence that it discourages promotion wars.

4. *Objective and task method*—This method consists of determining a budget by defining objectives, determining the tasks required to meet those objectives, and estimating the associated costs. The advantage of this method is that it requires management to iterate its assumptions about the relationship between money spent and

expected activity. This is normally the preferred method for a practice to use in determining its promotion budget.

Determining the Promotion Mix

Practices face the task of distributing the total budget for promotion among the various components. There are many factors that influence the distribution of the promotion budget and the nature of the promotional tools used.

Public relations activities often seem more credible than advertisements and can dramatize a practice's offerings. Such activities are typically an underused resource that can have great benefits. Writing a column for a monthly newsletter published by a hospital or health care payer can be an effective promotion activity.

Personal contact is especially effective at the later stages of the buying process because it allows a relationship to be built. Engaging in public relations activities is most helpful for a practice seeking to increase awareness and develop credibility among the provider and consumer populations.

Some promotional tools are more effective than others, depending on the buyer's stage of readiness (see Figure 8). Advertising and publicity are more effective at the awareness stage. Knowledge is affected most by ad-

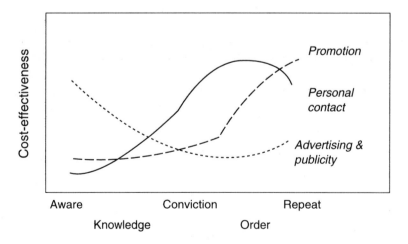

FIGURE 8   Cost-effectiveness of promotional tools versus buyer readiness. Adapted from *Marketing Management* (6th ed.; p. 613) by P. Kotler, 1988, Englewood Cliffs, NJ: Prentice-Hall. Copyright 1988 by Prentice-Hall. Adapted by permission.

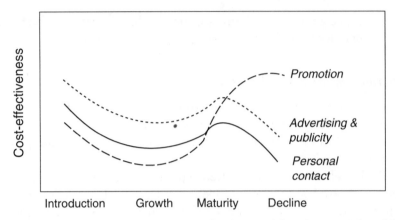

FIGURE 9 Cost-effectiveness of promotional tools versus life cycle stage. Adapted from *Marketing Management* (6th ed.; p. 614) by P. Kotler, 1988, Englewood Cliffs, NJ: Prentice-Hall. Copyright 1988 by Prentice-Hall. Adapted by permission.

vertising and personal selling. Conviction is influenced by personal selling, while promotion becomes more effective during the ordering and re-ordering stages. Advertising and publicity are more effective during the introductory and growth stages of a service, while promotion is more effective during the maturity and decline phases. This is illustrated in Figure 9.

STRATEGIES FOR INCREASING COMMUNICATION WITH PATIENTS

There is an increasing emphasis today on patient-provider communication. Patients want better communication with providers and they want it in lay terms. In this regard, psychologists may be the most skilled of all health care practitioners since their very livelihood is driven by effective consultation with patients. Nonetheless, the following list offers a few reminders that provide for an atmosphere for effective interaction:

- Do not hurry a patient; he or she is both a patient *and* a customer.
- Maintain eye contact with the patient and conduct active listening.
- Communicate on physically equal terms. Both the provider and patient should be sitting.
- Ask the patient if he or she has any other concerns.
- Do not interrupt a visit with a phone call unless absolutely necessary.

- Ensure that the patient understands at the end of each visit what has been accomplished and what is to be done if a follow-up visit is necessary.
- Provide oral and written instructions. When possible, include written educational material.
- Remind staff of the importance of telephone etiquette. They are the first and often last point of contact in a patient's visit.

Designing an Effective Advertising Program

Advertising is written communication. It is an important part of the marketing process. There are five major tasks involved in developing an advertising program:

1. What are the advertising objectives?
2. How much can be spent?
3. What message should be sent?
4. What media should be used?
5. How should the results be measured?

Setting the Advertising Objectives

The first step in developing an advertising program is to set the advertising objectives. The objectives must be congruent with the decisions already made regarding the target market, market positioning, and marketing mix. An advertising goal is a specific communications task that is to be accomplished with a specific audience. Advertising objectives can be classified in three ways according to their aim: to inform, persuade, or remind.

1. *Informational Objectives*—Telling patients about a new service.
   Describing available services.
   Correcting false impressions.
   Reducing patients' fears.
   Building a practice's image.
2. *Persuading objectives*—Building practice preference/reputation.
   Persuading referral sources to receive information.
3. *Reminding objectives*—Reminding patients the service may be needed in the near future.
   Reminding patients where the practice is located.
   Maintaining the practice's public profile.

Deciding on an Advertising Budget

After a practice has determined its advertising objectives, it can proceed to establish an advertising budget. The role of advertising is to increase demand for the practice's services. If a practice spends too little on advertising, the effect will not be the desired one. Conversely, if a practice spends too much on advertising, some of the money will be wasted. There are several factors to consider when setting an advertising budget:

1. *Life cycle stage*—New practices need to build awareness and gain customers. Established practices usually have lower advertising budgets.
2. *Market share*—Practices with high market share usually require less advertising than those with a lower market share. Building market share requires more advertising.
3. *Competition*—A practice must advertise its services more if there are a large number of competitors and high advertising expenditures.
4. *Advertising frequency*—Some messages need repetition, so frequency also is a factor in the decision-making process.
5. *Service substitutability*—Services that are considered a commodity require more advertising to establish a differential image. Also, advertising is important when a practice can offer unique benefits or has unique features.

Deciding on the Advertising Message

Creativity is important when determining an advertising message. There are three main steps in developing a creative strategy: message generation, message evaluation and selection, and message execution.

A practice's message should be determined as part of developing the service concept because it expresses the major benefit of the practice's services. Within this concept, however, there is latitude for a number of messages. Consumers are a major source of ideas. Their opinions about the strengths and weaknesses of existing services provide a practice with important clues on developing a message.

Messages should be evaluated according to such criteria as desirability, exclusiveness, and believability. A message should first say something desirable or interesting about the practice. Next, it should say something distinctive that no other practice offers. Finally, the message must be believable. The impact a message has depends not only on what is said but how it is said. The tone, style, wording, and format should deliver a cohesive message and image. The picture and headline must summarize the selling proposition.

Deciding on the Media

The next step in the advertising process is to choose the appropriate advertising medium to deliver the message. Media selection involves finding the most cost-effective medium to deliver the desired message to the target audience. In addition, a practice must decide on its desired reach, frequency, impact, media types, media vehicles, and timing.

A macroscheduling problem with media timing is that of scheduling the advertising in relation to seasonal and business cycle trends. If a practice has seasonal trends, it can choose to advertise in sync with its high season, opposite its high season, or year round. Mailings to school counselors in the fall, to pastors at Christmas time, to hospital social workers in February, and to juvenile justice officials in the summer are all examples of seasonal advertising.

A microscheduling problem is that of allocating advertising expenditures within a short period to obtain the maximum impact. Advertising can be done in bursts, can be dispersed continuously, or can be dispersed imtermittently. The timing decision should consider three factors: buyer turnover (the higher the turnover rate, the more frequent the advertising should be); the purchase frequency (the higher the purchase frequency, the more frequent the advertising should be); and the "forgetting" rate (the higher the rate at which the audience forgets an advertisement, the more frequent it should be). A practice that focuses on long-term therapy, for example, should advertise more often than a practice that tests children in the fall.

Measuring a Campaign's Success

By adding up the planned campaign costs, the needed break-even response rate can be determined in advance. By carefully analyzing past campaigns, a practice can steadily improve its performance. Even when a specific campaign fails to break even, it might still be profitable in the long run.

Ultimately, a campaign's success should not be measured strictly in terms of revenue but, rather, in terms of the *relationships* developed. Most practitioners would be pleased to be a person's family practitioner for a lifetime, but first the patient must try the services. Thus, a practice's follow-up efforts should include communications that do not attempt to "sell" services but rather to maintain the patient's interest in the practice and its offerings. Such communications include newsletters, lifestyle tips, and holiday greetings, all serving to build a stronger patient relationship.

SPECIFIC PROMOTIONAL TOOLS

Developing a Yellow Pages Advertisement

A *Yellow Pages* ad can be an effective advertising tool. The phone book is an often-used information source and may be particularly relevant in selecting behavioral health services because people may be unwilling to solicit information face to face or even over the phone. The *Yellow Pages* provide a completely anonymous source for an individual seeking practice information.

A graphic artist can assist in developing an ad. *Yellow Page* ad sales representatives also can help but understand that their primary job is to sell the most expensive ad possible.

Practices developing their own ads should first decide on the information they want to include. The information should be short and to the point. The layout should be clean and professional looking. Consider including the following information:

- Simple headline to gain attention
- Name of practice
- Names of providers
- Address
- Phone number
- Office hours
- Specialties
- Any special services (evening hours, multilingual, free parking)
- Border to separate the ad from others
- Directions or a small map

The letterhead, typeface, and symbols used in the advertisement should be consistent with a practice's other literature. In addition, some providers like to include a picture. It may also help to use a phrase or sentence that differentiates the ad from others. The size of the advertisement is at the discretion of the practice. Obviously, the larger the ad, the more attention people will pay it. It is important, however, to stay within the norms set by the local community. A practice may not want to run a full-page ad in a community where the other providers have only one-line listings. Finally, before approving an ad, check it carefully, since it will be in print for an entire year.

Developing a Practice Brochure

A brochure is a good way to inform current and potential patients about a practice. A brochure should not only inform people about a practice's services but also state the practice's principles, detail its policies and procedures, and reflect concern for the patients. A practice might consider including the following information in a brochure:

- A "thank you" to the patients for their trust and confidence in the practice.
- A statement on the practice's philosophy of behavioral health services.
- Address, phone number, fax number, office hours, directions, map, and emergency number.
- Services and specialties offered.
- Procedures for making an appointment, what to do in an emergency.
- How fees are set, how insurance is handled, how collections are handled.
- Synopsis of providers' qualifications.

A practice may hire a company to print the brochures or may reproduce them in-house. Brochures can then be mailed to prospective patients seeking further information. A practice might also display some brochures in the office, to be picked up by patients in the reception area.

Promoting a Practice Through Community Involvement

Providers can:

- Volunteer for public service activities and events, such as the United Way Campaign, American Red Cross blood drives, or local walks for AIDS research.

- Join civic organizations, such as the Lions Club.
- Participate in community planning sessions or local government meetings.
- Offer pro-bono services after traumatic events or disasters.
- Plan or attend local social functions.
- Assist local scouting or religious youth organizations.
- Write articles, editorials, or behavioral health tips for the local newspaper.
- Help television stations verify health information or do public service announcements.

Direct Marketing

Direct marketing and public relations programs are often viewed as secondary to advertising but can contribute greatly to a practice's marketing efforts. Since these marketing methods have not been widely understood or utilized, a practitioner who learns to use them more effectively can gain a competitive advantage in the marketplace.

Although direct marketing was first used in the form of direct mail and mail-order catalogs, it has been adapted to many forms in recent years. These methods include telemarketing, direct-response radio and television, and the Internet. The common thread among these marketing vehicles is that they are all designed to disseminate information directly to targeted and prospective patients and to obtain information from these groups as well. By contrast, mass advertising reaches an unspecified number of people, most of whom are not in the market for psychological products or services and will not make a purchasing decision regarding such services until some future occasion.

While direct marketing has enjoyed increased popularity, many practices still relegate it to a minor role in their promotion mix. Many advertising agencies do not offer direct-marketing services because they are unfamiliar with the methods and because they make more money developing and running advertising campaigns.

Direct marketing is an interactive system of marketing that uses one or more media to effect a specific response. Many users of direct marketing visualize it playing a broader role in their businesses, a role called direct-relationship marketing. Through the use of direct-response advertising, media marketers can learn much about potential clients in their geographic areas. Names and profile information are entered in a patient database that is used to build a continuing and enriching relationship with the behavioral health care provider. The emphasis is on building preferred patient relationships. Many service industries, including airlines, hotels, and retailers, are building strong client relationships through interactions with customers in their databases. The client database allows them to target their offers and information to those customers and prospects who are most willing, able, and ready to purchase their products or services. To the extent that they succeed, they gain much higher response rates to their promotions.

Sales through direct-marketing channels have grown rapidly. While retail sales grow at a rate of approximately 6% annually, direct-marketing sales are growing at a rate of about 10%. Some direct-marketing methods that are particularly applicable to psychological services are direct-mail marketing; television direct-response marketing; and radio, magazine, and newspaper direct-response marketing.

Direct-mail marketers send single mail pieces—letters, flyers, foldouts, and other materials. Some direct marketers mail audiotapes, videotapes, and even computer diskettes. As technology makes its way into American households, interactive media are becoming increasingly popular. A computer diskette could allow a potential patient, payer, or referral source to move through a menu of choices to view the data that are most relevant and/or important. Potential menus include persuasive copy, biographical or professional background information, graphical depictions of providers and/or facilities, and answers to frequently asked questions.

In general, direct-mail marketers hope to promote services, collect or qualify leading contacts, or communicate interesting news. Names may be selected from a list compiled by the practice itself or from lists purchased from mailing list brokers. These brokers have lists of every description, segmented on the basis of a variety of factors. Direct marketers typically purchase a subsample of names from a potential list and perform a test mailing to determine if the response rate is high enough.

Direct mail is popular because it permits high target-market selectivity and can be flexible and personalized. Direct mail has been very successful in promoting everything from books to insurance to industrial items. The direct-marketing methods described below may prove most effective for marketers of psychological services.

Cable TV is a growing marketing medium. Direct-response marketers air television spots that persuasively describe a product or service and give customers a toll-free number to call. Callers can receive additional information about products, can arrange appointments, and are questioned for responses that are included in informational databases.

Magazines, newspapers, and radio also are used to present direct-response offerings to customers, who hear or read about products or services and respond to a toll-free number or pull-out response card to learn more about the services.

Direct marketing provides a number of advantages to behavioral health practices. It allows greater prospect selectivity. Practices can buy mailing lists that contain the names of almost any group. Messages can be personalized and customized. Furthermore, a practice can build a continuous relationship with each patient. Direct marketing can be timed more precisely to reach prospects at the right moment. Direct-marketing materials receive higher readership, since they reach more interested prospects. Direct marketing also permits privacy in that the direct marketer's offer and strategy are not visible to competitors. Finally, a practice knows whether its advertising campaign has been successful because of response measurement.

Database marketing goes far beyond direct marketing by using sophisticated analytical techniques to target groups of individuals. It is important not to confuse a customer list with a marketing database. A customer list is simply a set of names, addresses, and telephone numbers, whereas a marketing database contains individuals' demographics, psychographics, past revenues, and other relevant descriptors.

In preparing a direct-marketing campaign, practices must decide their objectives, targets, offering strategy, various tests, and measures of campaign success. These decisions are reviewed below.

Psychology practices normally aim to secure immediate requests for services from prospective patients. A campaign's success is judged by its response rate. A response rate of 2% is normally considered good in direct-marketing sales campaigns. Additionally, a direct-marketing effort presumably has an effect on some people's awareness of and intention to seek services at some later date. Furthermore, not all direct marketing is designed to produce immediate sales. Direct-marketing efforts may also produce prospective patient lists and strengthen practice image.

A great advantage of direct marketing is the ability to test under real market conditions the efficacy of different components of the offering strategy. Direct marketers can test product or service features, copy, prices, media, mailing lists, and the like. Although direct-marketing response rates are usually at the single-digit level, testing these components can add substantially to overall response rate and success.

The response rate to a direct-marketing campaign typically understates the long-term impact of the campaign. Although only 2 to 5% of recipients may respond to a particular mailing, a much larger percentage of recipients becomes aware of that which is being advertised (direct mail has high readership), and some percentage of those recipients form an intention to buy the product or service at a later date. Furthermore, recipients might mention the product or service to others as a result of seeing the promotion.

Public Relations

Public relations (PR) is another important marketing tool. The public is defined as any group that has an actual or potential interest or impact on a practice's ability to achieve its objectives. Good PR can enhance a practice's image, which can improve patients' perceptions of quality, which translates into practice growth.

The public can facilitate or impede a practice's ability to achieve its objectives. The wise practice takes concrete steps to manage successful relations with its key publics, especially referral sources. If negative publicity occurs, the practice must act as a troubleshooter to diffuse the problem and effectively communicate with the concerned publics. The best PR efforts help practices adopt positive programs and eliminate questionable practices so that negative publicity does not arise in the first place.

Public relations activities can potentially impact public awareness at a fraction of the cost of advertising. Some experts say that consumers are five times more likely to be influenced by editorial copy than by advertising.

Major Decisions in Marketing PR

In considering when and how to use PR, a practice should establish its marketing objectives, choose its PR messages and vehicles, and evaluate the results.

Establishing Marketing Objectives

Public relations can effectively contribute to the following objectives:

- *Build awareness*—Place stories in the media to bring attention to the practice, its services, people, or ideas.

- *Build credibility*—Add credibility by communicating the message in an editorial context.
- *Stimulate external drivers*—Boost enthusiasm among publics that provide clients and complementary services.
- *Hold down promotion costs*—PR costs less than direct mail and media advertising. The smaller a practice's promotion budget, the stronger the case for using PR.

Choosing the PR Message and Vehicles

A practice interested in pursuing public relations activities must identify or develop interesting stories to tell about its services. Do any of the psychologists or staff members have unusual backgrounds, or are they involved in unusual or interesting projects? Taking the time to explore these avenues will usually uncover a number of interesting stories that can be used in press releases or literature relating to the practice. The stories chosen should reflect the image that the practice wants to reflect.

If the number or type of stories is insufficient, inappropriate, or otherwise impractical, the practice should consider sponsoring newsworthy events. Here the challenge is to create news rather than find news. Ideas include hosting or participating in academic conventions; inviting expert speakers; and participating in local forums, workshops, and health fairs.

Implementing the PR Plan

Implementing publicity requires care. For example, placing a great story in the news media is relatively easy, but most stories are somewhat less than great and may not get past busy editors. Staging special events also requires a great deal of preplanning and attention to detail. Sponsors of such events should be prepared with quick solutions to the many contingencies that can arise.

Evaluating PR Results

When PR is used in conjunction with other promotional tools, its contribution is hard to measure. Goodwill is often difficult to quantify or evaluate in terms of its impact on daily operations. Still, several methods of measurement are available for PR efforts.

The easiest measure of PR effectiveness is the number of exposures carried by the news media. The number of newsprint lines or minutes of air time can be quantified in terms of estimated audiences and valued as purchased advertising. This method fails to indicate how many people actually read, heard about, or recalled the message and what they thought afterward. There is no information on the net audience reached, since publications overlap in readership. Because publicity's goal is reach not frequency, it would be useful to know the number of unduplicated exposures.

A better measure is the change in awareness, comprehension, or attitude that results from the PR campaign (after allowing for the effects of other promotional tools).

- How many people recall hearing the news item?
- How many told others about it?
- How many changed their minds after hearing it?

All these questions lead to answers about the true effectiveness of public relations efforts. Effective PR tools for psychological practices include publications and public-service activities.

Practices rely extensively on communications materials to reach and influence their target markets. These include brochures, articles, audiovisual materials, and newsletters. Brochures can play an important role in informing target customers about what services are offered and who is offering them. Thoughtful articles written by members of a practice can draw attention to the practice and its services through employer newsletters or health plan mailings. Audiovisual materials such as films and audio and videocassettes are commonly used as promotional tools. The cost of audiovisual materials is usually greater than the cost of printed materials, but so is the impact.

Practices can improve public goodwill by contributing money and time to good causes. Supporting community affairs in the neighborhood where the practice is located is a good technique. Donating personal time and interest in local projects and charities can build goodwill for a practice while accomplishing broader objectives.

SUMMARY

The promotional tools that practices can use to communicate their service offerings include advertisements, sales promotions, public relations, personal contacts, and direct marketing. The six steps involved in developing an effective communications (promotion) strategy are (1) identifying the target audience, (2) determining the communication objective,

(3) designing the message, (4) selecting the communication channels, (5) allocating the budget, and (6) deciding on the promotion mix. Public relations, an important communication tool, includes publications and public-service activities.

CASE STUDY
Martin Clinic Promotes Its Services

Martin Clinic has evaluated several options for promoting its services and has adopted the action plan outlined below:

Advertising

The professional staff agreed that advertising services would not support the confidential atmosphere that the clinic's clientele seek. However, the *Yellow Pages* listing will be modified to include reference to the PPOs with which the clinic is affiliated. A budget item for increasing the size of the listing was approved. Additionally, the practice's brochure will be updated to include the new psychologist's name and background as well as photographs of each professional.

Promotion

Martin Clinic will provide staff and other support to health fairs organized by the PPOs it is affiliated with or the local hospital. A clinic professional will call or visit with each physician who has made a referral to the practice in the past year to express the clinic's appreciation. A budget was established to support sending an appropriate "thank you" to the high school counselors in recognition of their continued support. The possibility of sponsoring continuing education for the counselors will be explored.

Public Relations

The clinic will provide a quarterly article to each of the PPOs to consider for inclusion in their membership newsletters. The following topics were approved for this purpose:

- How to identify the early warning signs of alcohol abuse in teenagers.
- The effects of alcohol consumption during pregnancy.
- Talking to children about illegal drugs.
- Encouraging children to say "no" to drugs.

- Additionally, the clinic approved language for a letter to each of the county officials explaining why the clinic would not participate in a contract offering if one is forthcoming.

  Personal contact and direct marketing were determined not to be suitable for this practice, its clientele, and community.

6

Organizing and Implementing
Marketing Programs

T HIS CHAPTER PROVIDES *a sample marketing plan; the administrative tasks involved in marketing; and a discussion of how to organize, implement, and evaluate marketing activities. It explores ways in which a practice can grow, a practice's ethical and social responsibilities, and when a practice needs help marketing.*

SAMPLE MARKETING PLAN

The culmination of a practice's analysis of its market is the development of an overall marketing strategy in the formation of a marketing plan that incorporates the "four Ps" (product/service, price, promotion, place). The following page contains a sample marketing plan.

ORGANIZING THE MARKETING FUNCTION

The complex changes in the health care delivery market have driven changes in the marketing function as well. Marketing has evolved from a simple function to a complex group of activities, not always well integrated with each other or in relation to a practice's nonmarketing activities. Most small and mid-sized psychology practices will not require a separate marketing staff; however, all practices start out with five simple functions that must be managed and controlled. Someone must raise capital (finance), hire people (personnel), provide services (operations), sell the services (sales), and keep the books (accounting). Some practitioners may prefer to solicit third-party agencies to perform a number of these functions. Larger, more integrated practices may benefit from controlling these

Spears and Associates	
Marketing Goal	Increase client retention.
Market Research	The practice has recently experienced a large number of requests to transfer records to other practices. The practice surveyed patients and discovered that: 70% of families have both spouses working, 50% consider its office hours to be inconvenient, 50% have difficulty scheduling appointments in a reasonable time period, and 60% say the office's appearance is not positive.
Target Market	Current patients who may be dissatisfied and considering another practice.

Need	Strategy
Product	
More convenient hours	Evaluate adding evening hours to accommodate working family members. Leave schedule open in early morning and late afternoon to work in hard-to-schedule patients.
Less waiting time	Review scheduling policies. Review check-in procedures.
More time with provider	Reevaluate approach with patients. Make time with patients as productive as possible.
Appointments scheduled within 2 weeks	Consider expanding office hours.
More attractive office appearance	Replace furniture, carpet, and wallcoverings.
Price	
Need to understand that both spouses work	Revise fee schedule; acknowledge that appointments may result in lost wages.
Place/Distribution	
More convenient appointments	Evaluate access to office location. Parking lot is often full.
Promotion	
More information about practice	Develop practice brochure. Mail letter to patients and referral sources announcing new office hours.

functions internally. Regardless, marketing research and advertising are part of the sales function that must be addressed.

MARKETING IMPLEMENTATION

How can those charged with implementing marketing plans be most effective? A brilliant strategic marketing plan counts for little if it is not implemented properly. Marketing implementation is the process that turns marketing plans into actions and ensures that such actions are taken in ways that accomplish the plan's stated objectives.

Whereas strategy addresses the what and why of marketing activities, implementation addresses the who, where, when, and how. Strategy and implementation are closely related in that one level of strategy implies certain tactical implementation actions at a lower level. Four skills are related to effective implementation of marketing programs: skill in recognizing and diagnosing problems, skill in assessing the practice level (where the problem exists), skill in implementing plans, and skill in evaluating implementation results.

Diagnostic Skills

The close interrelationship between strategy and implementation can pose difficult diagnostic problems when marketing programs do not fulfill their expectations. Were the outcomes the result of poor strategy or poor implementation? The issues of determining what the problem is (diagnosis) and what should be done about it (action) are most pressing. Each problem calls for specific management tools and solutions.

Practice Levels

Marketing implementation problems can occur at three levels. One level is that of carrying out the marketing function successfully. Another level is that of implementing a marketing program that must blend many marketing functions into a coherent whole (as when introducing new services into the market). A third level is that of implementing marketing policy. For example, there must be consistent handling of patients by all members and levels of the staff.

Marketing Implementation Skills

Four skills must be practiced at each level within an organization to achieve effective implementation:

1. *Allocating*—Used by practices in budgeting resources (time, personnel, money) to functions, programs, and policies.
2. *Monitoring*—Used in managing a system of controls to evaluate the results of marketing actions.
3. *Organizing*—Used in developing an effective working organization. Understanding the formal and informal members of the staff who have input in or influence on the marketing function is important to effective implementation.
4. *Interacting*—Refers to the ability of marketers to get things done by influencing others. This includes people inside and outside the practice. Market research firms, ad agencies, and other agents may have objectives that differ from those of the practice.

EVALUATING AND CONTROLLING MARKETING PERFORMANCE

A practice must plan and control its marketing activities. Because surprises will occur during the implementation of marketing plans, the person responsible for marketing activities must continuously monitor and control those activities. Many practices have inadequate or nonexistent control procedures.

An annual plan control can create an implementation plan that ensures it achieves the revenue, profits, and other goals established in its annual plan. Four steps are involved in managing a plan by objectives:

1. The practice sets monthly or quarterly goals.
2. The practice monitors its performance in the marketplace.
3. The practice determines the causes of serious performance deviations.
4. The practice takes corrective action to close the gaps between its goals and performance. This could require changing the action programs or even changing the goals.

TOOLS TO MONITOR MARKETING PLAN PERFORMANCE

Several tools are available to assist practices in monitoring marketing plan performance:

- *Revenue analysis* measures and evaluates actual patient fees compared to patient revenue goals.

- *Market share analysis* reveals how well a practice is performing relative to its competitors. In general terms, if market share increases, the practice is gaining on its competitors; if it goes down, the practice is losing relative to its competitors. A number of assumptions qualify market share analysis. To be most effective, market share analysis should evaluate a practice's performance against that of its closest competitors in size, service, location, and other relevant factors.
- *Customer satisfaction tracking* is a qualitative control measure that is often more important than financial and quantitative measures. Given the highly personal and interactive nature of psychological services, customer satisfaction is a necessary qualitative measure that provides early warnings to the management of impending market share changes. Practices should develop systems to monitor the attitudes and satisfaction levels of patients and other stakeholders in their practices. By monitoring changing levels of customer preference and satisfaction, management can take early action when problems occur. This conduit for feedback should be viewed as a constructive part of any practice.

Ways to Grow a Practice

There are several ways to grow a psychology practice, including the following:

- Attract new patients.
- Encourage existing patients to purchase additional or different services.
- Encourage existing patients to purchase higher-value services.
- Increase client retention and loyalty.

The marketing efforts of many practices emphasize attracting new customers, but a well-managed practice will work hard to retain its current patients as well. It is more expensive to attract a new customer than retain a current one. Obviously, it is important in the behavioral health profession to maintain high ethical and professional standards. Maintaining professional conduct does not preclude marketing activities, however, and can actually enhance a practice both in terms of the quality of the services provided (because marketing requires a practice to identify and meet its patients' desires) and its profitability.

A *Practice's* Ethical and Social Responsibilities

Practices need to ultimately evaluate whether they are practicing ethical and socially responsible marketing. A practice's business success is intimately tied to the adoption and implementation of high standards of business and marketing conduct. By assessing the quality of a practice's performance along ethical and social responsibility lines, marketing efforts are most likely to follow the same high standards of action.

When a Practice Needs Help Marketing Itself

Marketing a psychology practice may appear to be a daunting task. The marketing process does require time and effort on the part of providers. But as health care trends are evolving, it is becoming more and more necessary for practices to market themselves in order to survive. Practices may consider hiring an outside consultant to lead their marketing effort. It may be useful to hire a graphic artist or an advertising agency to assist in designing a logo, brochure, or *Yellow Pages* ad. Also, if a practice has never done any kind of strategic planning or marketing planning and is either in danger of closing or wishes to substantially expand, it might consider contacting a consulting firm. A practice should look for a consultant who is experienced in the behavioral health field and in marketing small businesses. Other sources that may be helpful in assisting a practice in marketing itself are local college/university small business development centers, the Small Business Administration, or local community development offices.

SUMMARY

A marketing plan is the culmination of the marketing strategy. It states the marketing goal, gives the results of the marketing research, and lists strategies for each of the four Ps that relate to meeting the specific goals. Implementation is the process of turning marketing plans into actions. Implementation addresses the who, where, when, and how of the marketing plan.

A practice may do much of the marketing effort itself but may want to consider using a graphic artist or advertising agency for assistance in logo development, practice brochures, and *Yellow Pages* ads. A practice might also consider using consultants when its survival is threatened, if it has never done strategic or marketing planning, or when it wants to expand dramatically. Local college/university small business development centers, the Small Business Administration and local community development offices can be additional sources for marketing assistance.

CASE STUDY
Martin Clinic Implements Its Marketing Program

Reviewing the Martin Clinic's marketing process to date:
The forecast has shown that demand exists to support an additional 1.8 professionals in the practice.

With respect to market segmentation, client surveys indicate a strong preference for a highly confidential, caring atmosphere. Approximately 85% of the clientele have behavioral health insurance coverage and half of those fall under a PPO agreement that the clinic has negotiated.

The target market is patients who are insured through one of the PPO groups with which the clinic is affiliated.

The Martin Clinic's market strategy is to differentiate itself along two factors:

- Competence (specializing in adolescent substance abuse)
- Confidentiality (private records with no potential for public access)

The overall marketing mix of the practice was determined to be:
- *Product/service*—Adolescent substance abuse, with priority given to potential patients served by one of the contracted PPOs.
- *Pricing*—The clinic shall abide by the terms of the PPO contracts. For noncontract patients the clinic will maintain a fee schedule that is 20% higher than the highest PPO allowance. The clinic will continue to accept Medicare and Medicaid patients as a public service.
- *Promotion*—The clinic will work through its PPOs to promote its services.
- *Place*—The clinic will modify the interior space of its offices to provide privacy to all professionals and their patients.

Each of the marketing mix action items approved by the clinic is summarized in an action plan to simplify tracking of responsibilities.

Marketing Action Plan

Task	Responsible Personnel	Taget Date	Completion Date
Meet with *Yellow Pages* representative to discuss layout and cost of larger ad	A	Feb. 1	
Hire graphic artist to create ad	A	Feb. 15	
Approve ad at staff meeting	A, B, C, D, E	March 15	
Place ad	A	March 20	
Have professional photos taken for practice brochure	A, B, C, D, E	Feb. 15	
Hire printer to update practice brochure	B	Feb. 15	
Write letter volunteering for PPO health fairs	C	March 1	
Contact other health care providers who have made referrals (personal or phone)	A, B, C, D, E	June 1	
Send thank-you gift to school counselors for their continued support	C	April 1	
Explore sponsoring contin- ued education for counselors	C	April 1	
Write quarterly article for each PPO's newsletter	B, C, D, E	Feb. 1, April 1, July 1, Oct. 1	
Write letter to county officials explaining why the clinic would not participate in the county contract	E	Feb. 1	

The success of Martin Clinic's marketing program will be evaluated on a quarterly basis using the following indicators:

- Total number of new clients referred to the clinic
- Total number of new clients accepted
- Percentage of new clients with PPO coverage
- Total number of clients per professional
- Total number of sessions per professional

Glossary

ACCESS   Patients' ability to obtain needed health services. Measures of access include the location of health facilities and their hours of operation, patient travel time and distance to health facilities, the availability of medical services, and the cost of care.

CAPITATION   Method of payment for health care services in which the provider accepts a fixed amount of payment per subscriber, per period of time, in return for specified services over a specified period of time.

CARRIER   Any commercial insurance company.

CARVE OUT   An arrangement in which coverage for a specific category of services (e.g., mental health/substance abuse, vision care, prescription drugs) is provided through a contract with a separate set of providers. The contract may specify certain payment and utilization management arrangements.

CASE MANAGEMENT   Monitoring, planning, and coordination of treatment rendered to patients with conditions that are expected to require high cost or extensive services. Case management is focused and longitudinal, usually following the patient for 3 to 6 months minimum to avoid hsopital readmission.

Central Processing Unit (CPU)   The computer's brain, which largely determines the speed and cost of hardware.

CLAIMS REVIEW   A review of claims by government, medical foundations, professional review organizations, insurers, or others responsible for payment to determine liability and amount of payment.

CONCURRENT REVIEW   Third party review of the medical necessity, level of care, length of stay, appropriateness of services, and discharge plan for a patient in a health care facility. Occurs at the time the patient is treated.

CONTINUUM OF CARE   In behavioral health, generally defined as the spectrum of care delivered in residential treatment, inpatient, partial hospitalization, home health, and outpatient settings.

COPAYMENT   Type of cost sharing whereby insured or covered person pays a specified flat fee per unit of service or unit of time (e.g., $10 per office visit, $25 per inpatient hospital day); insurance covers the remainder of the cost.

COST CONTAINMENT   Actions taken by employers and insurers to curtail health care costs (e.g., increasing employee cost sharing, requiring second opinions, preadmission screening).

COST SHARING   Requirement that health care consumers contribute to their own medical care costs through deductibles and coinsurance or copayments.

CREDENTIALING   Process of reviewing a practitioner's credentials (i.e., training, experience, demonstrated ability) for the purpose of determining whether criteria for clinical privileges have been met.

DIAGNOSTIC RELATED GROUPS (DRGs)   Reimbursement methodology whereby hospitals receive a fixed fee per patient based on the admitting diagnosis regardless of the length of stay or amount of services received.

ENROLLMENT   Means by which a person establishes membership in a group insurance plan.

EXCESS CHARGES   Portion of any charge greater than the usual and prevailing charge for a service. A charge is "usual and prevailing" when it does not exceed the typical charge of the provider in the absence of insurance and when it is no greater than the general level of charges for comparable services and supplies made by other providers in the same area.

FEE FOR SERVICE   In the traditional fee-for-service model, the provider bills the patient or payer for a specified amount, typically on the basis of the amount of time spent delivering the service. Until recently, providers determined the fees charged for services and customary fees were generally accepted. Now, providers may be required to accept a payer's fee schedule, which demands that a certain fee be accepted as payment in full. PPOs represent an attempt to save the fee for service method of payment by regulating the cost of treatment in the context of a traditional reimbursement plan.

FEE SCHEDULE   A listing of accepted fees or predetermined monetary allowances for specified services and procedures.

FREE-STANDING FACILITY   Health care center that is physically separated from a hospital or other institution of which it is a legal part or with which it is affiliated, or an independently operated or owned private or public business or enterprise providing limited health care services or a range of services, such as ambulatory surgery, hemodialysis treatment, diagnostic tests, or examinations.

GATEKEEPING   Process by which a primary care provider directly provides primary care to patients and coordinates all diagnostic testing and specialty referrals required for patients' medical care. Referrals must be preauthorized by the gatekeeper unless there is an emergency. Gatekeeping is a subset of the functions of a primary provider's case manager.

GROUP CONTRACT   Arrangement between a managed care company and subscribing group that contains rates, performance covenants, relationships among parties, schedule of benefits, and other conditions. The term is generally limited to a 12-month period but may be renewed.

GROUP PRACTICE   A group of practitioners organized as a private partnership, limited liability company, or corporation; participating practitioners share facilities and personnel as well as the earnings from their practice. The providers who make up a practice may represent either a single specialty or a range of specialties.

HEALTH MAINTENANCE ORGANIZATION (HMO)   Health care delivery system that provides comprehensive health services to an enrolled population frequently for a prepaid fixed (capitated) payment, although other payment arrangements can be made. The organization consists of a network of health care providers rendering a wide range of health services and assumes the financial risks of providing these services. Enrollees generally are not reimbursed for care provided outside the HMO network.

INDEMNITY INSURANCE PLAN   An insurance plan that pays specific dollar amounts to an insured individual for specific services and procedures without guaranteeing complete coverage for the full cost of health care services.

INDIVIDUAL PRACTICE ASSOCIATION (IPA) MODEL HMO   An organization that contracts with individual health care professionals to provide services in their own offices for enrollees of a health plan. Specialists are generally paid on a fee-for-service basis, but primary care providers may receive capitated payments.

INTEGRATED CARE   Alternative health care delivery system developed by the American Psychological Association in response to the rising cost of providing health care services. It is based on six concepts: Benefit Design, Case Management and Utilization Review, Communications, Direct Contracting, Network Development, and Outcomes.

INTEGRATED DELIVERY SYSTEM   (IDS) System of behavioral health care that offers "one-stop shopping" to potential payers, meaning that a payer can write one check for the entire delivery of care without having to independently negotiate terms with multiple unconnected providers. IDSs offer a full continuum of care, so patients and premiums are managed within one accountable plan's network of providers.

LEVERAGE   A managed care strategy for controlling costs by steering patients to lower-cost providers called substitutes. In behavioral health care, a clinical social worker's psychiatric nurse may be a substitute for a psychologist.

MANAGED CARE   A means of providing health care services in a defined network of health care providers who are given the responsibility to manage and provide quality, cost-effective care. Increasingly, the term is being used by many analysts to include (in addition to HMOs) PPOs and even forms of indemnity insurance coverage that incorporate preadmission certification and other utilization controls.

MENTAL HEALTH AND DRUG ABUSE SERVICES   There are three basic types of mental health services: inpatient care provided in short term psychiatric units in a general hospital or specialized psychiatric facility; outpatient care for individual or group counseling; and partial hospitalization, a combination of both of the above. See also Employee Assistance Program.

MONITOR   The video display portion of a computer system.

MSO   An entity that usually contracts with practitioner groups, independent practice associations, and medical foundations to provide a range of services required in medical practices, such as accounting, utilization review, and staffing.

MULTISPECIALTY GROUP   Group of doctors who represent various specialties and work together in a group practice.

NETWORK   Group of providers who mutually contract with carriers or employers to provide health care services to participants in a specified managed care plan. A contract determines the payment method and rates, utilization controls, and target utilization rates by plan participants.

NETWORKING   To conect computer systems electronically so that users may share files or printers.

PEER REVIEW   Evaluation by practicing providers (or other qualified professionals) of the quality and efficiency of services ordered or performed by other practicing providers. Medical practices, inpatient hospital and extended care facility analyses, utilization reviews, medical audits, ambulatory care, and claims reviews are all aspects of peer review.

PER DIEM   Negotiated daily rate for delivery of all inpatient hospital services provided in one day regardless of the actual services provided. Per diems can also be developed by the type of care provided (e.g., one per diem rate for adult mental health, a different rate for adolescent substance abuse treatment).

PERFORMANCE STANDARDS   Standards that an individual provider is expected to meet, especially with respect to quality of care. The standards may define the volume of care delivered in a specified time period.

PERIPHERALS Optional hardware devices that can be connected to a computer system via cables (e.g., a printer).

POOL   A large number of small groups or individuals who are analyzed and rated as a single large group for insurance purposes. A risk pool may be any account that attempts to find the claims liability for a group with a common denominator.

PREADMISSION REVIEW   When a provider requests that a patient be hospitalized, another opinion may be sought by the insurer. The second provider reviews the treatment plan, evaluates the patient's condition, and confirms the request for admission or recommends another course of action. Similar to second opinions on surgery.

PREAUTHORIZATION   Review and approval of covered benefits, based on a provider's treatment plan. Some insurers require preauthorization for certain high-cost procedures. Others apply the preauthorization requirement when charges exceed a specified dollar amount.

PRECERTIFICATION   Review of the necessity and length of a recommended hospital stay. Often, certification prior to admission is required for nonemergencies and within 48 hours of admission for emergency treatment.

PREFERRED PROVIDER ORGANIZATION   (PPO) Selective contracting agreement with a specified network of health care providers at reduced or negotiated payment rates. In exchange for reduced rates, providers frequently receive expedited claims payments and/or a reasonably predictable market share of patients. Employees may have financial incentives to utilize PPO providers.

PROVIDER   Health care professional (or facility) licensed to provide one or more health care services to patients.

PROVIDER-HOSPITAL ORGANIZATION   Vertically integrated delivery system formed by practitioners and a hospital.

QUALITY ASSURANCE   Activities and programs intended to ensure the quality of care in a defined medical setting or program. Such programs include methods for documenting clinical practice, educational components intended to remedy identified deficiencies in quality, as well as the components necessary to identify and correct such deficiencies (such as peer or utilization review), and a formal process to assess a program's own effectiveness.

QUALITY MANAGEMENT   A participative intervention in which employees and managers continuously review the quality of the services they provide. The process identifies problems, tests solutions to those problems, and constantly monitors solutions for improvement.

REQUEST FOR PROPOSAL (RFP)   Formal document soliciting bids from system vendors.

RISK   The chance or possibility of loss. Risk sharing is often employed as a utilization control mechanism in HMOs. Risk is often defined in insurance terms as the possibility of loss associated with a given population.

SELECTIVE CONTRACTING   Negotiation by third-party payers of a limited number of contracts with health care professionals and facilities in a given service area. Preferential reimbursement practices and/or benefits are then offered to patients seeking care from these providers.

SOFTWARE   Computer programs used to instruct computer hardware on how to perform.

STAFF MODEL HMO   An HMO in which professional providers in a multispecialty group are salaried employees of the HMO.

SUBSTITUTE   A provider who replaces another despite differences in training and licensing scope. A clinical social worker and a psychiatric nurse may be substitutes for each other.

SUPPORT   Assistance provided by a computer vendor after a sale, including training, maintenance, and trouble-shooting.

THIRD PARTY ADMINISTRATOR   Outside company responsible for handling claims and performing administrative tasks associated with health insurance plan maintenance.

THIRD-PARTY PAYER   An organization that pays or insures health care expenses on behalf of beneficiaries or recipients who pay premiums for such coverage.

USUAL, CUSTOMARY, AND REASONABLE (UCR)   Charges considered reasonable and that do not exceed those customarily charged for the same service by other providers in the area.

UTILIZATION REVIEW   Independent determination of whether health care services are appropriate and medically necessary on a prospective, concurrent, and/or retrospective basis to ensure that appropriate and necessary services are provided. Frequently used to curtail the provision of inappropriate services and/or to ensure that services are provided in the most cost-effective manner.

VALUE-BASED PURCHASING   Selection of a product or service based on criteria other than unit price. Value criteria may include quality, outcome, and access.

Bibliography

Bleiler, E. H. (1987). *Medical Economics Practice Management Problem Solver #1*. Oradell, NJ: Medical Economics Books.

Brown, S. W., & Morley, A. P. (1986). *Marketing Strategies for Physicians: A Guide to Practice Growth*. Oradell, NJ: Medical Economics Books.

Chiama, E. T. (1992). Value marketing in your group practice. *Medical Group Management Journal, 39*(4), 27–31.

Connor, R. A., Jr., & Davidson, J. P. (1985). *Marketing Your Consulting and Professional Services*. New York: John Wiley & Sons.

Diamond, S. L., & Berkowitz, E. N. (1990). Effective marketing: A road map for health care providers. *The Journal of Medical Practice Management, 5*(3), 197–203.

Eldredge, M. B. (1992). Marketing plans for physicians' practices. *Journal of Ambulatory Care Management, 15*(2), 19–28.

Eliscu, A. T. (1992). Marketing your practice through community involvement. *Medical Group Management Journal, 39*(4), 35–37.

Fisk, T. A. (1990). Creating patient satisfaction and loyalty. *Journal of Health Care Marketing, 10*(2), 5–15.

France, K. R., & Grover, R. (1992). What is the health care product? *Journal of Health Care Marketing, 12*(2), 31–38.

Gerson, H. J., Brauner, N., & Goldman, E. F. (1988). Strategic pricing. Build a market-oriented pricing strategy. Factors for Success. *Healthcare Executive Magazine, May/June*, 27–31.

Gilbert, F. W., Lumpkin, J. R., & Dant, R. P. (1992). Adaptation and customer expectations of health care options. *Journal of Health Care Marketing, 12*(3), 46–55.

Javalgi, R., Joseph, W. B., Gombeski, W., & Lester, J. (1993). How physicians make referrals. *Journal of Health Care Marketing*, 26–35.

Kotler, P. (1988). *Marketing management* (6th ed.). Englewood Cliffs, NJ: Prentice-Hall.

Kotler, P. (1992). *Marketing management* (8th ed.). Englewood Cliffs, NJ: Prentice-Hall.

Luallin, M., & Sullivan, S. (1992). Medical marketing: Yesterday, today, tomorrow. *Medical Group Management Journal, 39*(4), 19–24.

Maister, D. H. (1991). How clients choose. *Professional Service Firm Management*, 57–63.

Maister, D. H. (1991). Quality work doesn't mean quality service. *Professional Service Firm Management*, 66–71.

Maister, D. H. (1991). A service quality program. *Professional Service Firm Management*, 73–84.

Parrington, M., & Stove, B. (1991). The marketing decade: A desktop view. *Journal of Health Care Marketing, 11*(1), 27–32.

Personett, A., & Fyfe, A. (1988). Market segment management: An alternative to product line management. *1988 Health Care Marketing Review,* 57–60.

Press, I., Ganey, R. F., & Malone, M. P. (1991). Satisfied patients can spell financial well-being. *Journal of Health Care Marketing, 10*(2), 5–15.

Scammon, D. L., & Smith, J. A. (1989). A marketing approach to planning mental health care services. *Journal of Ambulatory Care Management, 12*(3), 61–68.

Schwisow, C. R. (1992). Using specialty advertising in a niche marketing plan. *Medical Group Management Journal, 39*(4), 32–33.

Sullivan, K. W., & Luallin, M. D. (1989). The medical marketer's guide: Success strategies for group practice management. Englewood, CO: Medical Group Management Association.

Swinney, A. (1989). Relationship marketing: Reviving the fine art of wooing. *The Academy Bulletin,* 56–57.

Tombetta, W. L. (1989). Channel systems: An idea whose time has come in health care marketing. *Journal of Health Care Marketing, 9*(3), 26–35.

Waldman, A. (1995). Psychiatric marketing undergoes many changes. *Healthcare Marketing Report, 13*(3), 1–5.

Wold, C. R. (1992). *Managing Your Medical Practice.* New York: Times Mirror Books.